ILLUSTRATED LIVES
OF THE
SAINTS

ILLUSTRATED LIVES
OF THE
SAINTS

John McNeill

Crescent Books
New York/Avenel, New Jersey

This 1995 edition published by Crescent Books,
distributed by Random House Value Publishing, Inc.,
40 Engelhard Avenue,
Avenel, New Jersey 07001

Random House
New York · Toronto · London · Sydney· Auckland

Produced by Brompton Books Corporation,
15 Sherwood Place,
Greenwich, Connecticut 06830

ISBN 1-517-12183-2

8 7 6 5 4 3 2 1

Printed and bound in The Czech Republic

PAGE 1
St. Thomas Aquinas, detail of the Demidoff
altarpiece by Carlo Crivelli, 1476.

PAGE 2
St. Clare, panel painting in the convent of Sta
Chiara, Assisi, *c.*1300, showing the saint with
scenes from her life.

PAGE 3
St. Guthlac sailing to Crowland to establish his
monastic retreat there, from the late twelfth-
century *Guthlac Roll.*

RIGHT
St. George and the Dragon by the nineteenth-
century English painter Sir Edward Poynter.

Contents

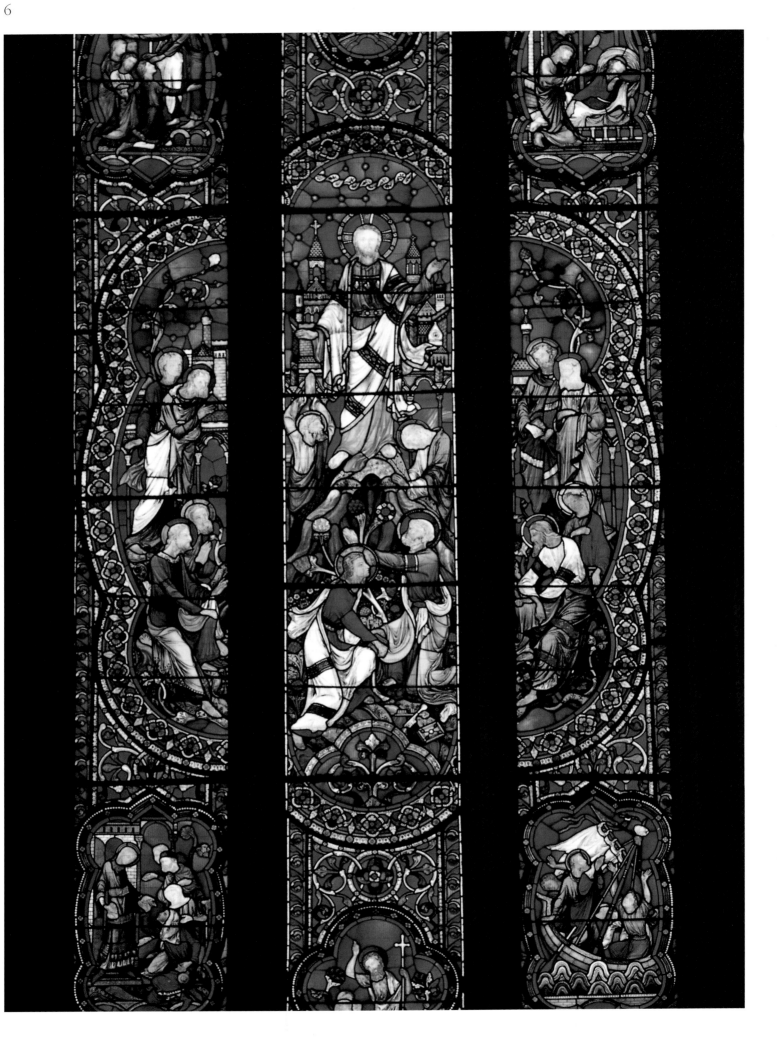

Introduction

Saints occupy a peculiar place in society. In its original usage, the Latin term *sanctus* signified holy, specifically devoted to God, set apart. It might refer to both objects and people, and it did not, at least not until recently, indicate a stainless character or high moral tone, simply a holiness, or sacredness to God. This idea of separateness, of the individual devoting his or her life to God, or being specially favored by Him, invests the saint with what might be described as metaphysical power, with insights into the nature of Being, and supernatural abilities transmitted through the Holy Spirit. Thus saints do not belong to any particular category of society, but rather occupy a place somewhere between this world and God. It is this which gives saints their fascination to the historian of the Middle Ages; they bubble up through the strata of an acutely conventional society, take precedence over popes and kings, becoming rallying points for popular devotion. Above all, they cannot be brought low by persecution, for their martyrdom is the kiss of a new life.

The veneration of saints has an ancient pedigree, and rests on the belief that since the saint is human and, being favored by God, must now be in Heaven, he or she might intercede on behalf of the living. The *Martyrium Polycarpi* of *c.*156 maintains that Polycarp's disciples held a feast in his honor on the anniversary of his martyrdom. Although the early martyr cults borrowed much from pagan funerary rites, the anniversary they celebrated was not the terrestrial birthday of the deceased, but their arrival in Heaven, i.e. their death. Initially these feasts were celebrated at the grave of the martyr, and were thus purely local, but by the third century one hears of the practice of dismembering the body of the saint so as to distribute relics more widely, and of the enshrinement of secondary relics, such as strips of cloth, which had been in contact with the body of the martyr. By this date Christians also began to travel to visit the shrines of martyrs, or those places in the Holy Land associated with the life of Christ. Helena, Constantine's mother, undertook a pilgrimage to Bethlehem and Jerusalem in 325, and was followed in the late fourth century by Jerome and the Spanish nun Etheria, whose account of her journeys, the *Peregrinatio Etheriae*, recounts visits to shrines in Egypt, the Holy Land, Asia Minor and Constantinople.

Virtually all early saints were martyrs, but after Constantine granted the Church a legal identity in the 313 Edict of Milan, the persecutions abated. A second group of saints then began to attract public veneration. To distinguish these figures from the martyrs, they were honored by the term *confessor*, meaning that they bore witness to Christ through their enduring confession of the Christian faith. The great teachers and ascetics were so honored, figures such as Ambrose, Jerome, Simeon Stylites and Martin of Tours, and the distinction between martyr and confessor, while not rigid, seems to have held a meaning for the early Christian communities of Europe. Gregory of Tours, writing in the late sixth century, epitomized this in his composition of two

LEFT: Christ in Heaven surrounded by saints. Hereford Cathedral.

RIGHT: SS Luke and Peter, from a thirteenth-century Salzburg lectionary.

anthologies of saints' lives; the *Glory of the Confessors* and *Glory of the Martyrs*.

The methods whereby an individual might be sainted varied, both historically and geographically, but there are two essentials which indicate an acceptance of sainthood. The first is popular acclaim; any saint must be so called *per viam cultus*, by way of a cult. In the early Church this took the form of a spontaneous outpouring of devotion at the grave, which, if maintained on the anniversary of the death over a number of years, constituted a cult. Subsequently the cult might spread, either through a distribution of relics, or through the dedication of churches and altars to the saint. The second prerequisite is that the name of the saint should be entered in a list, or canon, hence the term canonization. This was usually done locally; by the fourth century bishops began to exercise a loose control over the process by consenting to the celebration of an annual feast in honor of the saint, in other words guaranteeing observation of the anniversary of the saint's death. As Christians began collating local canons to produce more general lists of feasts, local cults began to spread, and a more universal calendar took shape.

The institution of papal canonization is a late development, first encountered in 993, when Pope John XV acclaimed Ulrich of Augsburg a saint and added his name to the *Roman Martyrology*. Thereafter, papal approval was frequently sought as a means of legitimizing new candidates for the rank of sainthood. It was also felt that this offered some sort of protection against the proliferation of false cults, a useful safeguard in an increasingly saint-obsessed early medieval society. Nonetheless, it was not until *c*.1170 that Pope Alexander III decreed that no individual might be venerated as a saint without the approval of the Church of Rome, an initiative which became widely accepted during the papacy of Innocent III (1199-1216). Although intended to prevent abuses, concentrating the process of canonization in Rome made it no less vulnerable to aggressive petitions, or personal whim, and while extremely popular cult figures such as Osmund of Salisbury failed to win papal approval, purely political candidates, such as Edward the Confessor, were sainted. The actual procedures evolved slowly, but by the later Middle Ages the establishment of a papal commission was standard, charged with investigating the life of the candidate. If this was found to be exemplary, the commission would then pass on to consider the reported miracles. This obviously had an impact on the writing of saints' lives, for anxious cathedral chapters would often commission a life of their hoped-for saint from a leading writer, with a view to impressing the papal commission. The life would be presented as without moral stain; and the miracles would carry the names of witnesses. The formal process of canonization was to all intents and purposes a reversal of medieval priorities, for what mattered in the matter of popular devotion were miracles; the life was for inspirational stories.

Before passing on to the main text, a few practical observations should be made. I have included short lives of 100 saints, each entry arranged alphabetically for ease of reference. As the Church has at various times recognized well over 10 000 saints, and sanctions the Feast of All Saints (November 1), in honor of those it has not individually sainted and who are known only to God, this is but a small selection. The criteria adopted in making a choice were neither rigorous nor historical, and they essentially reflect a personal bias. About half of those included might be regarded as Universal Saints, that is to say their cult was widely celebrated in both the Eastern and Western Churches. The other half enjoyed more local cults, and their inclusion was motivated out of a desire for variety, either in terms of the type of cult they generated, or the nature of the lives they led. Wherever possible I have included references to the earliest known source material, and indicated the date at which this might have been written. The illustrations are in many ways the most important element of the book, for taken as a whole they say something about how saints came to be perceived, the miracles they worked, their position in an ecclesiastical hierarchy, and their promise. For saints, like angels, offer a connection between the world of the palpably mundane and the eternity of a world to come.

Without the interest and goodwill of colleagues and friends, this volume would have been impossible to write. I should particularly like to thank the staff of the British Library for their help in locating some of the more obscure source material, and my students for their patient forbearance as I became immersed in a heady mixture of hagiography, pilgrimage, cult imagery and story-telling. That I was even encouraged to do so came as a bonus. Kusuma Barnett, Shirley Liffen and Gale Thomas were extremely generous in their support, and I was touched by the style and sympathy with which they conjured up lives of Olaf, Alban and Catherine. To them I owe a considerable debt. I should also like to single out Malcolm Armstrong, Ian Dunn, Roger Norris, Brian O'Callaghan and Barbara Vossel for the practical and conversational stimulus they offered the book.

The greatest debt is owed to those who taught me to appreciate medieval history and art in the first place. Their ideas and methods permeated any thinking I entertained on the subject of sainthood, and I wish to take this opportunity to thank Joanna Cannon, Eric Fernie, Lindy Grant, Sandy Heslop, Peter Kidson, Andrew Martindale and John Mitchell for their efforts to equip me with a little understanding. The flaws and omissions are entirely mine. Finally, I should like to thank my editor, Jessica Hodge, and picture researcher, Suzanne O'Farrell, for managing the project with such convivial ease. The book is dedicated to Anthony Gibbs, whose inventions could match the finest within these covers.

ABOVE: The Three Magi, from a twelfth-century English psalter.
BELOW LEFT: Seventeenth-century saints' altarpieces in Notre-Dame-
des-Cordeliers, Laval, France.
RIGHT: Simeon the Stylite on a sixth-century reliquary.

Aethelwold *c.908-84*
Monk and bishop Feast day August 1

Born at Winchester, Aethelwold was taken into the household of Athelstan, King of Wessex, probably while still quite young. Aethelwold was ordained priest by Aelfheah, Bishop of Winchester, on the same day as **Dunstan**, and between *c.*940 and 954 served as a monk at Glastonbury while Dunstan was abbot. His request to leave Glastonbury to work under the reforming abbot Aymard at Cluny (Burgundy) was refused by King Eadred, and instead, in 954, he was asked to restore the lapsed abbey of Abingdon (Oxfordshire). While there he invited "skilled chanters" from the abbey of Corbie (Picardy) to join the community, and sent Osgar, one of the monks, to study the monastic customs of Fleury (St-Benoît-sur-Loire). These initiatives probably postdated Dunstan's return from exile at St. Peter's, Ghent, in 957, but are the earliest evidence for the adoption of the continental reform in Anglo-Saxon England.

Aethelwold's appointment as Bishop of Winchester in 963 completed the groundwork necessary to ensure the monastic reform took root, for with Oswald in charge of both Worcester and York, and Dunstan at Canterbury, the senior English bishoprics were in the hands of like-minded men. In 964 Aethelwold took the dramatic step of throwing the secular canons out of Winchester Cathedral, replacing them with a congregation of Benedictine monks. Two years later he did the same at the New Minster, Winchester, and followed this up by founding or re-founding the great Fenland abbeys of Peterborough, Ely, Thorney and Crowland. Aethelwold's practical abilities, both as an administrator and as an artist, were remarkable. He is recorded as a cook at Glastonbury, a bell-founder at Abingdon, and a mason at Winchester, and his foundation of a monastic scriptorium at the Old Minster, Winchester, was responsible for the growth of one of the most significant centers of book production in medieval Europe.

Aethelwold's most celebrated achievement was his hosting of the 973 Council of Winchester, in concert with Oswald, Dunstan and King Edgar. The Council was responsible for drawing up the *Regularis Concordia*, a set of liturgical customs which were to be observed in all English monastic houses. In effect the *Regularis* codified the aims of the monastic reform; by describing

the offices to be sung on each day of the year, and the principal liturgical areas of the church, and by defining the relations between a monastic chapter and its royal benefactors, it became the backbone of English monastic life for the next century.

Agatha *Third century?*
Virgin and martyr Feast day February 5

The earliest surviving mention of Agatha is in Jerome's *Martyrology*, and the importance of the cult is attested by the foundation of two churches under her dedication in sixth-century Rome and one in sixth-century Ravenna. She is also featured in the Procession of Virgins on the north wall of Sant' Apollinare Nuovo, Ravenna, of *c.*561. The later accounts of her life are pure invention, however. According to these she came from a wealthy Sicilian family, and as a Christian took a vow of virginity. Her beauty attracted the attention of the consul Quintinian, but she rejected him and so in punish-

ABOVE: *Benedictional of St. Aethelwold*. The miniature represents a bishop, possibly Aethelwold himself, pronouncing a blessing. A poem written in gold at the opening of the manuscript states that the Benedictional was made for Aethelwold's own use by Godeman, one of the Winchester monks, and the reference to miracles witnessed at the shrine of St. Swithun in 971 suggests it was written between 971 and Aethelwold's death in 984. The Benedictional consists of a collection of texts used by a bishop when blessing the congregation during the Mass.

ment she was handed over to the strikingly named brothel-keeper, Aphrodisia, who failed to corrupt her. Quintinian then invoked an Imperial edict aimed against Christians and had her tortured, the gruesome ordeals almost matching those inflicted on St. George in their brutality, featuring rods, racks, fire and shears. Finally her breasts were cut off, and she died in prison in Catania of her injuries. This last indignity gave rise to the attribute with which she is most commonly identified in medieval art, a platter on which are displayed her severed breasts.

Alban *Third century?*
Martyr Feast day June 22

Alban is first mentioned in a mid-fifth-century life of Germanus of Auxerre by Constantius, and the story of his martyrdom was recounted by Gildas, in his *De Excidio* of *c.*516-47, and Bede, in his *Historia Ecclesiastica Gentis Anglorum* of *c.*716-31. Both suggest he was martyred in about 305, though modern scholars have argued his death was brought about under Septimus Severus, around 209. Either way, the fact of Alban's martyrdom is not in doubt, and as the earliest British martyr his cult acquired considerable importance during the Middle Ages.

The basic story is related by Bede. According to this, Alban was a Roman citizen living in Verulamium, who gave shelter to a Christian priest fleeing from persecution. Impressed by his faith, Alban converted and, having persuaded the priest to escape, donned his cloak and surrendered himself to the Roman authorities. Once it was realized Alban was not the original target but a respected Roman citizen, he was asked to make a sacrifice to the pagan gods. He refused and was flogged, after which his execution was ordered by the presiding judge. Alban was taken out of the town to the river Ver, but the crowds gathered on the bridge were so great that neither he, nor his captors, were able to cross. It was then that the miracles flowed. First, the river dried up to allow a

ABOVE: *The Martyrdom of St Agatha* by Giambattista Tiepolo.

LEFT: *St. Agatha* by Bernardino Luini. The cult of St. Agatha became particularly popular in post-medieval Italy, where a number of important Carmelite convents took her dedication. Luini's sixteenth-century visualization of the saint shows Agatha wearing a garland of flowers and holding her severed breasts.

passage, a spectacle which persuaded the executioner to throw down his sword and ask to die with Alban. Second, a spring suddenly appeared out of the hill beyond the river, from which Alban drank. Finally, as the sword fell on his neck, the second executioner lost his eyes, being unable to see the truth.

Alban was buried either in or near an established cemetery on the flower-covered hill where he fell, and began to attract a pilgrimage, with Germanus of Auxerre among the earlier visitors. Bede also maintains that a church was built above the grave, where many miracles occurred. The foundation of the abbey of St. Albans did not take place until 793, however, when Offa, King of Mercia, endowed a monastic church into which the relics of St. Alban were translated.

It seems likely that, by the ninth-century Danish invasions at least, the shrine was a popular draw, but the relics themselves became entangled in a number of ownership disputes, which the great thirteenth-century St. Albans chronicler, Matthew Paris, was

anxious to lay to rest. Matthew Paris was responsible for writing, and possibly illustrating, the lives of several Anglo-Saxon saints, **Wulfstan**, **Edward the Confessor**, and **Guthlac** among them. His *Life of St. Alban* is understandably the most closely argued, and relates how the relics of St. Alban were stolen by a Danish army in about 870 and removed to a monastery at Odense (Denmark), Alban himself permitting this theft because of the lax discipline of his own monastic community. Once the abbey of St. Albans had been reformed, he appeared in a vision to one of the monks, Egwin, telling him how he might retrieve the relics. Egwin travelled to Odense and presented himself at the monastery, asking to be received into the order. He rose to the position of sacrist, where it became his duty to guard the relics. One night, he bored a hole into the base of the reliquary casket, removed the relics, and gave them to a group of merchants for return to St. Albans. Claiming homesickness, Egwin then followed shortly afterwards.

In a second, fairly typical, tale of claim

ABOVE: *Life of St. Alban.* The abbey of St. Albans had the good fortune to number Matthew Paris, the great thirteenth-century chronicler and historian, among its monastic congregation. The Dublin manuscript illustrated here is thought by many scholars to be in his own hand. The illustrations were probably added by an assistant, although it is possible they were produced by Paris himself around 1230, comparatively early in his career. This tinted drawing shows the martyrdom of St. Alban, while the executioner, blind to the truth, duly loses his eyes.

and counter-claim, two manuscripts describe the relics' removal to Ely for safe-keeping, shortly before the Norman Conquest. Relations between the abbeys became strained after St. Albans was informed that the bones Ely eventually returned to them were not those of Alban, but a worth-less skeleton. The St. Albans version augments this with their abbot's reply; that they had anticipated the trick, and sent only decoy relics in the first place. Recent archaeological attempts to locate the original burial place of St. Alban have proved unsuccessful.

Alphege *c.954-1012*
Martyr Feast day April 19

One of the leading figures in the tenth-century English monastic reform movement, Alphege had the most revered cult at Canterbury Cathedral prior to the murder of **Thomas Becket** in 1170. Virtually all that is known of Alphege is derived from five mentions in the *Anglo-Saxon Chronicle*, and Osbern's *Vita* of *c.*1090. From these we learn that Alphege was a monk at Deerhurst (Gloucestershire), and that after a period of solitude in Somerset, he was appointed Abbot of Bath by **Dunstan**, though the latter claim should be viewed with scepticism. Thenceforth his rise was rapid. In 984 he was created Bishop of Winchester in succession to **Aethelwold**, who had been a driving force behind the monastic reform movements. In 994 he acted as chief negotiator for Ethelred the Unready in a council with Swein Forkbeard, and in 1005 he was consecrated Archbishop of Canterbury.

In September, 1011, a Danish army laid siege to Canterbury, capturing the city after the archdeacon, Aelfmaer, went over to the opposition. Alphege and anyone else of note were imprisoned, and the Danes demanded ransoms, a particularly vast sum being placed on the head of the Archbishop. By the spring of 1012 the prisoners were held at Greenwich, and, though smaller ransoms had been paid for the nobility, Alphege forbade his people to pay any more, presumably in sympathy with Kipling's dictum "once you have paid the Danegeld/you will never get rid of the Dane." Incensed at the news, and having recently looted a wine-ship, a party of drunken Danes killed Alphege by pelting him with the bones of an ox recently consumed at a feast. The body was initially buried at St. Paul's Cathedral, London, but King Cnut was sufficiently anxious to encourage reconciliation between Anglo-Saxons and Danes that he allowed the body to be translated to Canterbury, and the Archbishop was reunited with his cathedral in 1023.

Ambrose *c.339-97*
Bishop and Doctor of the Church
Feast day December 7

Born into an old Gallo-Roman senatorial family in Trier, Ambrose rose quickly through the ranks of the Roman administrative system to be appointed provincial

governor of Aemilia-Liguria in 370, whose seat was then at Milan. In common with the whole of late-fourth-century Mediterranean Europe, the church of Milan was embroiled in the dispute between Arian and Catholic Christians. On the death of the Arian bishop, Auxentius, in 374, Ambrose appealed for a peaceful election at the assembly called to decide a successor. Although he was undergoing training as a catechumen, Ambrose was not then a baptized Christian. He was therefore not unnaturally surprised at hearing his appeal interrupted by a voice crying "Ambrose for bishop." The cry was taken up by the assembly, Ambrose's objections were overruled, and he was simultaneously baptized, ordained and consecrated bishop on December 7, 374.

ABOVE: St. Alphege, in St. Mary's, Deerhurst.

RIGHT ABOVE: *The Four Doctors of the Church*, Jacob Jordaens. Bravura seventeeth-century altarpiece representing Ambrose, Gregory, Augustine and Jerome. Ambrose is to the left.

RIGHT BELOW: *St. Ambrose in his Study* (woodcut, printed in Basle, 1491). The scourge hanging from a bracket to the left of the saint's chair refers to the penance he imposed on Emperor Theodosius.

The early years of Ambrose's episcopate were taken up with theological study under the Roman scholar Simplicianus, who encouraged him to read the Early Christian Greek writers, a study which influenced the treatise on the nature of faith he wrote for the emperor Gratian in 377. Gratian's sudden demise in 383 brought Ambrose into contact with Imperial politics at the highest level, and he was responsible for persuading the new western emperor, Maximus, not to move against the eastern emperor Valentinian II, famously informing the latter that "the emperor is in the Church, not above it."

The wisdom and clarity of Ambrose's sermons were particularly valued by **Augustine of Hippo**, and indeed were partly responsible for Augustine's conversion, and they were also widely read during the later Middle Ages. His most influential work was *De Officiis Ministrorum*, an ambitious treatment of Christian ethics, while his contribution to the liturgy is underscored by the few, extremely beautiful, Latin hymns to survive from his pen.

Ion. Luyken. invenit et fecit.

Andrew *First century*
Apostle and martyr
Feast day November 30

Identified as the brother of Simon Peter in all four gospels, Andrew was one of the fishermen of Bethsaida who were the first apostles of Christ. According to John, Andrew was a disciple of John the Baptist when he first encountered Christ, and was responsible for introducing Peter to "the Messiah." He is invariably among the first four names in the gospel lists of the apostles, but is not granted as intimate a role as that of the "inner circle" of Peter, James and John. He plays a significant part only in the Feeding of the Five Thousand and as a go-between for the Greeks who wished to meet Christ at the Feast of Passover.

The surviving accounts of Andrew's life after Pentecost are persistent, but unreliable. Eusebius of Caesarea, writing between 303 and 323, maintains that he preached in

ABOVE: *Martyrdom of St. Andrew*, engraving by Jan Luyken. Eighteenth-century image of Andrew crucified on a saltire cross outside the city gates of Patras.

LEFT: Images of the apostles beside the instruments of their martyrdom were commonplace from the early thirteenth century onward, though the landscape setting and theatrical piety of the painting shown here is very much a characteristic of the seventeenth and eighteenth centuries.

Scythia, while the early-third-century *Acts of St Andrew* alleges he was crucified at Patras in Achaia (Greece). Gregory of Tours repeats much of this account in his *Glory of the Martyrs* of *c*.590, and speaks of the tomb at Patras:

On the day of his festival the Apostle Andrew works a great miracle, that is manna with the appearance of flour, and oil with the fragrance of nectar, which overflows from his tomb. In this way the fertility of the coming year is revealed. If only a little oil flows, the land will produce few crops; but if the oil is plentiful it signifies that the fields will produce many crops. For they say that in some years so much oil gushed from his tomb that a torrent flowed into the middle of the church.

It is by no means easy to reconcile this account with the fourth-century belief that Andrew had founded the church of Constantinople, nor the story that Emperor Constantius sacked Patras in 345 and removed the body of Andrew to the Church of the Holy Apostles in Constantinople.

What is clear, however, is that relics of St. Andrew were highly prized during the early Middle Ages. Justinian's rebuilding of the Church of the Holy Apostles after 532 was believed to have enshrined the saint's relics, but innumerable accounts of portions of the saint traveling around Latin Europe suggest that either the body in Constantinople was not entire, or that another body, or bodies, had been claimed as Andrew. Gregory of Tours mentions some relics of Andrew in sixth-century Burgundy, and the church of San Pedro de la Rúa at Estella (Spanish Navarre) cherished his shoulder blade, while, most famously, St. Regulus brought a portion of the saint to Scotland. The latter journey is recorded in a mid-twelfth-century document, and though it is historically untenable in the form it takes there, it is clearly based on an actual journey and endowment. Modern scholarship considers this to have taken place during the early eighth century. The story goes that Regulus brought some relics of Andrew to Fife as a gift, where they were received by Hungus, who endowed a monastery at Kilrimont to enshrine them which subsequently became known as St. Andrews. The document speaks of him as having come from Patras, which is unlikely, but it is possible that Regulus was sent with them from Constantinople as a diplomatic gift, or that they were brought from Hexham for safe-keeping. With this established, Andrew was adopted as the patron saint of Scotland.

The tradition that Andrew was crucified on a saltire cross (X) cannot be dated any earlier than the tenth century, when it is mentioned in Autun. The symbol was adopted in Scotland, where it became known as St. Andrew's cross, and is the emblem of Scotland on the Union Jack. Representations of such crucifixions are even later still, and only became common during the late Middle Ages.

Anne *First century*
Mother of the Virgin Mary
Feast day July 26

Anne's name is first encountered in the mid-second-century *Protoevangelium of James*, where Anne and her husband Joachim are described as an elderly and childless couple, to whom an angel appears and announces that Anne will bear a child, whose name shall be Mary. Subject to medieval embellishment, this remains the basic legend of Anne. The cult seems to have become established in the East in the fourth century, and began to assume a

ABOVE: As may be seen from this mid-fourteenth century panel painting, the association of Andrew with the saltire cross did not gain widespread acceptance until well into the fifteenth century. The panel originally formed part of a large polyptych, and was probably painted in Siena *c*.1340.

LEFT: Virgin Mary with SS Anne and Joachim (Istanbul, Kariye Camii), mosaic of *c*.1310 in what was the Chora monastery in Constantinople, showing the infant Virgin Mary with her parents.

BELOW: Crypt of Canterbury Cathedral looking east. Anselm's biographer, Eadmer, ascribes the new crypt and choir at Canterbury to Anselm, and makes it clear that these were partly financed by the demesne revenues of the see. Work cannot have begun before 1096, when Anselm appointed Ernulf prior, and as a later Canterbury chronicler, Gervase, attributes the majority of the work to Ernulf's priorate, the crypt was probably completed by 1107 at the latest. If one discounts the nave arrangements at Chartres Cathedral, Canterbury's is the largest medieval crypt in Europe.

greater importance with the emergence of the doctrine of the Immaculate Conception, probably during the seventh century. This asserted that, as the Virgin Mary was entirely without sin, she was protected by God from the very moment of conception in Anne's womb. The doctrine was popular in England, where the Anglo-Saxon monk Eadmer of Canterbury wrote a treatise in its defence in about 1100, but it was by no means universally accepted throughout the West, and both the Cistercian and Dominican orders rejected it.

The apocryphal *Gospel of the Birth of the Virgin* lies behind the explosion of interest in Anne during the Middle Ages, and was clearly intended to feed that tremendous hunger for stories of Holy Childhood which seems, initially, to emerge in early-twelfth-century England. This adds a number of details to the earlier narratives, and tells of how Anne and Joachim divided their income into three equal portions, for the Temple, the poor, and for themselves, re-spectively. This was why they were chosen by God to bring the Virgin Mary into the world. The *Gospel* also maintains that Anne and Joachim surrendered Mary to the Temple at the age of three, and that Mary returned to their house in Nazareth after her

betrothal to Joseph, which was where the Annunciation took place. This is the basis for Giotto's pictorial account of Anne and Joachim on the south wall of the Arena chapel at Padua.

Anselm *c.1033-1109*
Archbishop Feast day April 21

Anselm was the son of a Lombard nobleman who, though born at Aosta (Italy), moved to Burgundy in 1056. He seems to have moved further north in 1059, drawn to Lanfranc's monastic school at Bec (Normandy), and completed his novitiate there the following year. He succeeded his mentor to the office of prior at Bec some time before Lanfranc's appointment as abbot of St-Etienne, Caen, in 1066. Anselm's earliest writings date from the period following his appointment as prior; the most significant is the *Proslogion*, famous for its argument that if God is that beyond which "nothing greater can be conceived," then any denial of God is a contradiction in terms (the "Ontological Argument"). This rigorous approach to theological discourse was refined in Anselm's later works, notably in his brilliant

ABOVE: *The Birth of the Virgin*, Pietro Lorenzetti. Representations of the birth of the Virgin to St. Anne, here seen in Pietro Lorenzetti's brilliantly realized interior of 1342, obviously borrowed some of the iconographical conventions of images of the birth of Christ.

Cur Deus Homo ("Why did God become Man?"), whose theories as to the reconciliation of humanity with God (Atonement) became the medieval standard. Modern historians are inclined to see in these writings the origins of scholastic philosophy.

Anselm's public career began with his election as abbot of Bec on the death of Herluin in 1078, and his subsequent elevation to the archbishopric of Canterbury in 1093. Anselm's predecessor, Lanfranc, had in fact died in 1089, but King William Rufus was anxious to keep the see vacant, and only consented to the election of Anselm, then in Chester, while suffering from a life-threatening illness. Anselm's consecration in December, 1093, ushered in a period of antagonism between Anselm and Rufus, over Canterbury's estates, rights of appointment to the bishoprics, and papal jurisdiction. Anselm eventually went into exile in 1097, and at the behest of Pope Urban II accompanied the papacy to Bari for the great council of October, 1098. Anselm's brief was to argue the position of the Latin Church over the dual procession of the Holy Spirit (the *Filioque* clause of the amended Nicene Creed), and so to persuade the Byzantine prelates of southern Italy into the Latin Church. Anselm's advocacy was successful, a triumph he may have felt would be followed by further successes after the Vatican Council of 1099 came out against lay investiture, but his recall to Canterbury by Henry I on Rufus' death in 1100 was unhappy. Anselm refused to do homage or consecrate Henry's chosen bishops, and after three years of arguments he reluctantly went to Rome to try to broker a compromise with the papacy. From 1103 to 1107 Anselm was once more in exile, and became something of a pawn in the dispute between the papacy and secular powers over rights of investiture. An extraordinary settlement was made without any reference to Anselm, in which no bishop was to be elected without Henry I's approval, and Anselm returned to Canterbury.

According to his biographer, Eadmer, Anselm died on April 21, 1109 "with the whole family of his children [the monks] gathered round him." His body was placed in the nave alongside the tomb of Lanfranc, and a local cult soon grew up. This was certainly the pretext for the translation of Anselm's relics into the chapel of SS Peter and Paul at Canterbury Cathedral on April 7, 1163, and later that year **Thomas Becket**

asked Pope Alexander III to initiate the canonization of Anselm. Anselm's claim seems to have been overlooked in the rush to canonize Becket in 1173, but the Canterbury chapel was known as St. Anselm's by 1185 at latest, and the feast of his death was widely celebrated in England and Flanders. He was formally recognized as a Doctor of the Church in 1720.

Anthony of Padua
1195-1231
Franciscan preacher Feast day June 13

Born in Lisbon and educated there at the cathedral school, Anthony attached himself in 1210 to the Augustinian canons, and from 1212-20 studied at the Augustinian priory in Coimbra (Portugal). The arrival at Coimbra of the bodies of several Franciscans mar-

tyred in Morocco seems to have precipitated a desire to become a preacher, and in
1220 Anthony joined the Franciscan order
and traveled to Ceuta (North Africa) to work
among the Moors. Illness forced his return,
and he made his way to Assisi in time to
attend the General Chapter of 1221. A later
vita maintains that a sermon he gave at Forlì
(Romagna) prompted St. **Francis** to appoint
him lecturer in theology to the entire order,
from which moment his rise was rapid.
Anthony taught at Bologna, Montpellier and
Toulouse, and was made Provincial of Emi-
lia-Romagna in 1227, responsible for the
supervision of all Franciscan friaries in the
area at a time of major expansion. He died
in 1231 at a convent of Poor Clares at Arcella,
just outside Padua.

His death was probably caused by ex-
haustion and excessive fasting, but despite
the brevity of his life a considerable num-

ber of Anthony's sermons survive. The two
principal collections, the *Sermons for Sun-
days* and *Sermons for Feast Days*, were
written between 1227 and his death. The
later accounts of his life also consider him
a miracle-worker, resurrecting still-born
children, persuading a mule to genuflect
before the consecrated host, even shocking
a student who had borrowed his psalter
into returning it, by appearing to him in a
minatory vision. His ability to work miracles
after his death is less conjectural, and there
is no shortage of reports from within a few
years of the translation of his body from
Arcella to the Franciscan friary in Padua.
This was accomplished in the teeth of opposition from Arcella, but following Anthony's
canonization in 1232 a new basilica was
built to house his tomb, dedicated to Sant'-
Antonio and variously refurbished between
the mid-thirteenth and late-sixteenth

ABOVE: *The Miracle of
the Mule*, Donatello.
This bronze relief is
one of four
commissioned from
Donatello for the high
altar of Sant' Antonio,
Padua, in 1446. It
represents the moment
when a mule rejects
the oats offered by the
two men standing to its
rear, and instead
genuflects before the
Host offered by St.
Anthony.

centuries. The growth of the church was a recognition of its emergence as one of the most popular reliquary centers of northern Italy, where it is known, more simply, as Il Santo.

Apollinaris of Ravenna
Date unknown
Bishop and martyr Feast day July 23

Apollinaris is first mentioned in a sermon of Peter Chysologus, Bishop of Ravenna (died *c*.450), who styles him a martyr. It is evident from the apse mosaic of Sant'Apollinare in Classe, in the old port of Ravenna, however, that by 549 Apollinaris was regarded as a

Bishop of Ravenna. Why this might be so is wrapped up in the ambitions of the Byzantine emperor, Justinian (527-65), and his archbishop, Maximian, for the newly created exarchate of Ravenna. Put simply, if Ravenna could demonstrate its august credentials as one of the earliest Christian bishoprics in Italy, and one which had metropolitan status, it might wrest ecclesiastical control of Emilia from Milan, and so bring Bologna into the Byzantine exarchate. The first Bishop of Ravenna to be granted metropolitan powers was none other than Peter Chrysologus, *c*.435, but the papacy was careful not to allow him to use the title archbishop, and in his cathedral he was a suffragan of Rome. In the masterly

BELOW: St. Apollinaris (Basilica of Sant' Apollinare in Classe, near Ravenna). The church of Sant' Apollinare in Classe was founded between 535 and 538 to house the relics of the saint. The apse mosaic would certainly have been completed in time for its consecration in 549, and shows Apollinaris flanked by twelve sheep, representing the apostles.

sixth-century mosaic in Classe, Sant'Apollinare is depicted wearing the pallium of an archbishop, and the man responsible for consecrating the church, Maximian, was the first to use the title.

As such, the identification of Apollinaris with Ravenna must have taken place before the first account of his life to survive was written. This, the *Passio S. Apollinaris*, seems to have been composed in the mid-seventh-century chancery of Archbishop Maurus in Ravenna, and maintains that Apollinaris was born in Antioch. After becoming a disciple of the Apostle Peter he traveled to Italy, where he was created first Bishop of Ravenna, but was thrown out of the city and stoned to death by a pagan mob.

Augustine of Canterbury
Died 604/5
Archbishop Feast day May 26

ABOVE: St. Apollinaris, detail of apse mosaic from the sixth-century church of Sant' Apollinare in Classe.

Previously a monk and then prior of the monastery of San Andrea, Rome, Augustine was chosen by Pope **Gregory the Great** in 596 to lead a mission to convert the English. The party consisted of between 25 and 40 monks, who hesitated while in Gaul but were successfully persuaded by Gregory to continue, and landed at Ebbsfleet (Kent) in the summer of 597. They were formally received at Canterbury by Ethelbert, King of Kent, who granted them a house in the city and awarded them the right to preach. Ethelbert's Frankish wife, Bertha, was already a Christian and had the use of the church of St. Martin, to the east of the city walls. For a while the new arrivals shared this church with Bertha but, though Ethelbert was not baptized until 601, he seems to have been sympathetic to the purposes of Augustine and his monks, and provided

LEFT: *Gospels of St. Augustine*. This sixth-century Italian gospel book is traditionally thought to have been brought to Canterbury by St. Augustine, a tradition with much circumstantial evidence in its favor. The manuscript was certainly used during the installation of archbishops of Canterbury from the early Middle Ages onward, a practice which continues today. The illustration shown here prefaces the *Gospel According to Luke*, and depicts scenes from the life of Christ.

RIGHT: *St. Augustine of Hippo in his Study*, Vittore Carpaccio. A popular late medieval tradition holds that Augustine was writing a letter to ask the advice of Ambrose on a theological matter, when his cell was filled with light. A voice from heaven then chastized him for his presumption, and informed him that Ambrose had just died. An edition of this apocryphal letter was published in Venice in 1485, and the story is clearly behind Carpaccio's superlative portrayal of 1502-08.

Augustine with an old Romano-British church in the center of the city to act as cathedral, probably in 598, followed by a grant of land. The earliest church on the site was dedicated to SS Peter and Paul, *c.*615, but was rededicated to St. Augustine by **Dunstan** in 978, by which title it was known throughout most of the Middle Ages.

According to Bede, "Augustine was buried outside but close to the church of the Apostles Peter and Paul, for it was not yet either finished or consecrated. But as soon as it was consecrated the body was carried inside and honorably buried in the chapel on the north side" (*Historia Ecclesiastica Gentis Anglorum*). Before Augustine's relics were translated into the new Anglo-Norman church in 1091, this northern chapel, or *porticus*, was the center of his cult. The impact of Augustine's mission on the later history of the English church can scarcely be overstated, for when Gregory originally despatched Augustine to England, his reading of Roman maps led him to propose that the two provincial centers should be in London and York. But with Augustine receiving the pallium of an archbishop in Canterbury, it was Canterbury which became the metropolitan center.

Augustine of Hippo
354-430
Bishop and Doctor of the Church
Feast day August 28

Augustine was born at Tagaste (North Africa) to a pagan father and a Christian mother, Monica, and received a Christian education, though remaining unbaptized. He was trained in rhetoric at the University of Carthage, but quickly abandoned his plans to graduate in the law and turned to the study of philosophy, simultaneously taking a mistress, with whom he was to live for 15 years, and by whom he had a son, Adeodatus. By this date he had renounced Christianity, and between 374 and 383 he professed himself a Manichaean. His disagreement with Faustus over the nature of the divine in man in turn led him to abandon Manichaeism, and late in 383 Augustine moved to Rome to establish a school of rhetoric. The school was short-lived, and he quickly moved north to take up a teaching appointment in Milan. Here he encountered **Ambrose**, the brilliant Gallo-Roman Bishop of Milan, whose sermons and biblical exegeses Augustine found both impres-

sive and persuasive. After long reflection at Cassiciacum, an inner dialogue superbly articulated in his *Confessions*, Augustine was baptized on Easter eve, 387.

He returned to North Africa in 388 and, with a number of companions, established a quasi-monastic community at Tagaste. He was ordained a priest in 391 and consecrated Coadjutor-Bishop of Hippo in 395, being elevated to the position of sole

Bishop of Hippo the following year. From 396 until his death on August 28, 430, Augustine lived communally with his cathedral clergy, preaching each Sunday and feast day, instructing cathechumens in the faith, caring for the poor, administering the diocese, presiding over civil and ecclesiastical disputes. The emphasis he laid on the pastoral responsibilities of a bishop were considered a model of episcopal governance by many contemporaries, and were to prove influential, but it is on his theological writings that the greater part of his reputation rests.

In these, his training in rhetoric was clearly important, and most of his work is polemical. The major issues he tackles – grace, charity, predestination and free will, original sin, the essential goodness of creation, sacramental validity – were refined in answer to the threat posed by the teachings of three major heretical movements. The most distant was that of the Manichaeans, whose roots were hardly Christian at all and with whom Augustine had personal experience on which to draw. But the most violent controversies were played out with the Donatists and Pelagians, and

Augustine's premise that the Church was unified through the charity of its members, and was "holy" not because any single Christian was or was not "good" but because the "purpose" of the Church was "holy", was widely accepted. His arguments against Pelagianism are more problematical, and formed the basis for his later teaching on original sin. They eventually led him into a position of extreme pessimism, little removed from predestinarianism, in which he argued that humankind is a *massa peccati*, one mass of sin, from which some souls have been elected to received divine mercy. One outcome of his position was that unbaptized babies are doomed to everlasting Hell.

Among his other writings are a number of epistles, the *Confessions*, several surviving letters from an electrifying correspondence with **Jerome**, and the magisterial *De Civitate Dei*. This last was written between 413 and 426; inspired by the fall of Rome to the Gothic chieftain, Alaric, in 410, it evolved a view of the relationship between Christianity and wordly empire which has been recognized as the main foundation for a Christian philosophy of history.

ABOVE: *Fantastic Ruins with St. Augustine and a Child*, by the seventeenth-century French painter François de Nomé. A rather charming medieval story maintains that as St. Augustine was walking along a beach he encountered a small boy trying to empty the ocean into a hole in the sand. Augustine rebuked him, saying "Thou attempts the impossible." The boy replied: "No more so than for thee to try to explain the mysteries of the Universe."

FAR RIGHT: *St. Barbara* by Robert Campin. The illustration shows the right wing of a triptych painted in 1438. The identification with Barbara rests solely on the tower, seen under construction through the window.

Barbara *Date unknown*
Virgin and martyr
Feast day December 4

Allegedly the virginal daughter of one Dios-corus, Barbara was martyred at some point between *c.*250 and *c.*313. Her legend first appears in a seventh-century Greek *Acta*, and she is included in the tenth-century *Menologion of Simeon Metaphrastes*, all of which makes an eastern Mediterranean origin for the cult likely, but the accounts were variously embellished in the Latin West during the Middle Ages. It seems likely that the legend was originally written as pious fiction. The essentials of the story are that Barbara was a maiden of unusual beauty, who was locked away in a tower by her father, Dioscorus, so that no man should gaze upon her. Her reputation still traveled, however, and a number of suitors petitioned for her hand in marriage. She be-came a Christian while her father was away on business, and on hearing of her conver-sion, Dioscorus denounced her to the Roman authorities. Dioscorus was ordered to kill her, which he managed to do, but was immediately struck by lightning and re-duced to cinders. The cult became immen-sely popular in late medieval France, and on the basis of her father's fate, Barbara was invoked as the patron of gunners and artillerymen.

Bartholomew *First century*
Apostle and martyr Feast day August 24

Identified as one of the twelve apostles in the synoptic gospels, Bartholomew's name means "son of Tolmai". Granted that this is a patronym, he may have been given a birth name also; where one would expect to find Bartholomew in the apostolic lists in John, the name Nathaniel is used:

And Nathaniel saith unto him, Can there any good thing come out of Nazareth? Philip saith unto him, Come and see. Jesus saw Nathaniel coming to him, and saith of him, Behold an Israelite indeed, in whom is no guile!

Scholars have long identified the two names as one person. Eusebius of Caesarea records a tradition that Bartholomew preached in India, while an early Roman tradition alleges he was martyred in Arme-nia, being first flayed alive and then beheaded. His relics were said to have been variously translated, passing through Bene-vento before being enshrined in the church

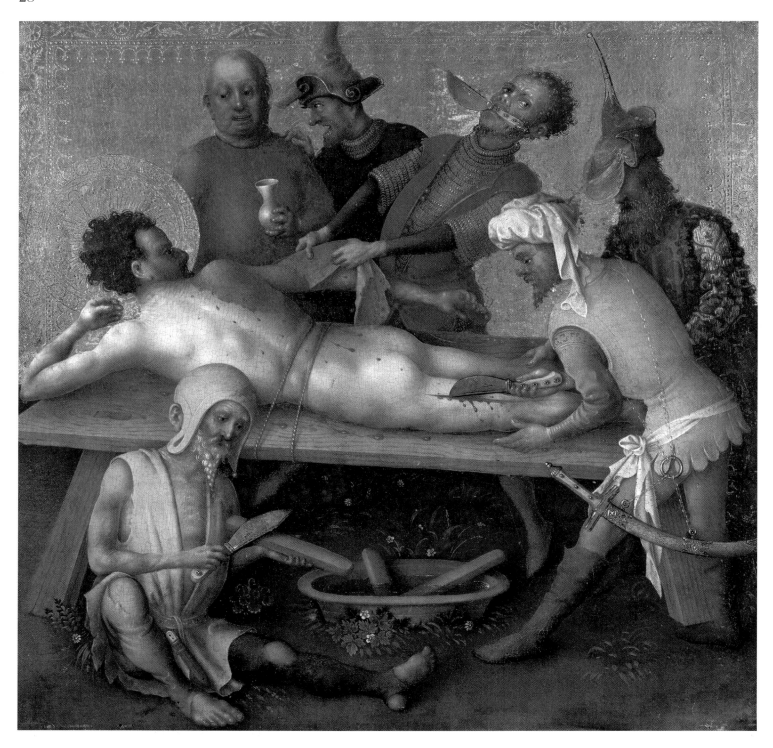

of San Bartolomeo, Rome. The cult was particularly popular in southern Italy and England, and owes its position in English calendars to the acquisition in the eleventh century of an arm of St. Bartholomew by Emma, second wife of Cnut, which she entrusted to Canterbury.

Basil the Great *c.330-79*

Bishop Feast day January 1 (East), January 2 (West)

Basil was born into a wealthy and well-established Christian family at Caesarea, and educated at Caesarea, Constantinople and Athens. His grandmother, parents, sister Macrina, and brother Gregory of Nyssa, were all subsequently venerated as saints. After a year spent in the early monasteries of Syria and Egypt, Basil retired in 358 to live as a hermit along the banks of the river Iris, near Neo-Caesarea. Here he was joined by the brilliant Capadocian theologian Gregory of Nazianzus, and began to develop his ideal of a monastic life which combined periods of contemplation with a duty to preach and care for the poor. Emperor Julian the Apostate, a student contemporary of Basil's in Athens, unsuccessfully tried to persuade him to join the court at Constanti-

ABOVE: *The Martyrdom of St. Bartholomew*, a panel by Stephan Lochner showing Bartholomew being prepared for flaying, a detail of Lochner's vast *Last Judgment* altarpiece of *c.*1440.

nople in about 362, but he did finally leave his hermit's cell in 364, after Eusebius, Bishop of Caesarea (a successor to the better known author of the *Ecclesiastical History*) demanded his help in combating the Arian policies of Emperor Valens. In 370 Basil was elected Bishop of Caesarea in succession to Eusebius.

The last decade of Basil's life was devoted to the care of his diocese, and to this end he established a complex of churches, hospitals and almshouses on the outskirts of Caesarea, a sizeable subsidiary town which became known as the Basiliad. His status as a metropolitan bishop also demanded that he play a prominent role in the Arian controversy, then raging within the Church. Basil's polemics against Eunomius, the leader of the extreme Arian party, represent him as an aggressive champion of orthodoxy, but are untypical of his writings in general. Indeed, his treatise *On the Holy Spirit* is a masterpiece of intellectual subtlety, and succeeded in bringing the semi-Arians into the orthodox fold, persuading them that their creedal description of the Holy Spirit, "like in substance to the Holy Father," inferred the Nicene "of one substance."

Basil is best known, however, for his monastic Rule, and thus as the father of eastern monasticism. The Basilian Rule survives in two versions, though both share the same basic character. The emphasis is on the communal, rather than the eremitical, life, and he stresses the need for a balanced regime of liturgical prayer, contemplation, manual work, and the care of the poor.

Benedict of Nursia
c.480-c.547
Founder of Benedictine monasticism.
Feast day March 21, moved to July 11 in 1969 to avoid Lent

The only early account of Benedict's life is contained in Book II of Gregory the Great's *Dialogues*, and though this can be supplemented with slightly later material, relatively little is known. He was born in Nursia (now Nórcia, Umbria) and educated in Rome, but became so disturbed by the rowdiness of the city that at the age of about 20 he left to take up the life of a hermit at Subiaco. In time disciples began to join him, and were eventually organized into 12 loosely eremitical communities. His success was not unmixed, however, and an

attempt was made on his life; a famous story whose principal ingredients, a poisoned chalice and a raven which removed the poison at Benedict's request, soon entered the medieval canon. This event may or may not have happened, but whatever the case it chimes with Benedict's disenchantment with life at Subiaco and in about 529 he moved with a small band of followers to Monte Cassino, where he established a monastery on the heights above the Roman Via Appia.

ABOVE: Late eleventh-century mosaic of St. Basil, from the church of Hosios Loukas at Phokis (Greece).

BELOW: Part of an early fifteenth-century predella by Lorenzo Monaco, showing St. Benedict admitting SS Maurus and Placidus into the community at Monte Cassino.

It was while he was at Monte Cassino that Benedict composed his Rule. All early monastic communities lived according to a Rule, each one individually tailored toward the needs of a particular community, and each purely local in application. Benedict's Rule was one among many, but it drew sensitively on the earlier prescriptions of **Basil**, John Cassian and Caesarius of Arles, and compared to most early monastic Rules is a model of clarity and good sense. The monks were to allot portions of each day for prayer, reading and manual work, these activities to be undertaken while they were not celebrating the Divine Office, which

was to be considered the principal task and central act of the monastic life. All possessions were to be held in common, and the monks were to elect a leader, or abbot, from among their own number. The vow required stability of residence, monastic zeal, and absolute obedience to an all-powerful abbot, while the abbot in turn was to be learned, flexible, discreet, and to act as a true father to his charges.

It is unlikely that Benedict could have foreseen the wholesale adoption of this Rule in medieval Latin Europe, but its innate balance and simple humanity appealed to later generations of monks and exercised a profound influence on the development of medieval concepts of space, solitude and order. Some modern scholars are inclined to argue that **Gregory the Great** knew Benedict's Rule and instructed **Augustine of Canterbury** in its precepts, the monastery of St. Augustine at Canterbury thus becoming the first community of monks outside southern Italy to adopt the Rule. It is certainly the case that Anglo-Saxon England was in the forefront of this diffusion, and both Wilfrid and Willibrord took up the Benedictine Rule in the late seventh century. Its medieval importance dates from a systematic revision made by Benedict of Aniane after 779, and by the time it had been endorsed at the founding of Cluny in 910, it had gained the status of a universal Rule. Possession of the relics of St. Benedict has been a matter of passionate dispute between the monasteries of Monte Cassino and Fleury (St-Benoît-sur-Loire) since the late seventh century.

Bernard of Clairvaux
c.1090-1153
Abbot Feast day August 20

One of six sons born to Tescelin Sorrel, a minor Burgundian nobleman, at Fontaines, near Dijon (Burgundy), Bernard was educated by Augustinian canons at Châtillon-sur-Seine. In 1112 or 1113 he decided to embrace monasticism, and with some 30 companions joined the abbey of Cîteaux, then presided over by the English churchman, Stephen Harding. The expansion of the Cistercian order dates from this moment, and four new foundations were swiftly established, that at Clairvaux taking Bernard as abbot in 1115. Bernard's influence on Cistercian monasticism can scarcely be overstated, and under his guidance the order expanded at a quite staggering rate, each monastery dependent on the one from which it was founded. Rievaulx and Fountains (Yorkshire) were the first English daughter-houses of Clairvaux, both of them founded in 1132, and by Bernard's death in 1153 the Cistercian order had grown from a single community at Cîteaux to 343 monasteries in France, Spain, Italy, Germany, England, Scotland and Ireland.

The governing principles behind this growth were admirably simple. Each house was to be established in a remote solitude, free from distractions, and the monks were to devote themselves to a life of prayer and manual labor. The Chapter General at Cîteaux would legislate for the entire order, and its pronouncements were to be published in the form of Statutes. The Statutes compiled between *c.*1119 and 1152 reflect Bernard's concern that the monks' surroundings should be simple. They prohibit the use of precious metals or fine fabrics within the church, or the construction of bell-towers without. This may suggest the Statutes were primarily negative, but they were intended to function as a counterpart to Bernard's teachings on the spiritual responsibilities of the individual. According to this, each monk should reach forward to a knowledge of God by first learning to know himself. With self-knowledge he may then begin to perceive, through the faculty of Reason, how God bestows earthly blessings, and may finally ascend to a life of the Spirit, in which the

BELOW: Bernard of Clairvaux, St. Mary's, Shrewsbury. Detail from a stained glass window showing St. Bernard excommunicating a swarm of flies which had settled at the abbey of Foigny; thus demeaned, the flies fall dead. The glass is part of a larger cycle made for the Cistercian abbey of Altenberg (near Cologne) between 1505 and 1532, and was purchased by the Rev. Rowland in 1845, following its removal for safekeeping during the Napoleonic Wars, and he had it installed in the parish church of St. Mary's, Shrewsbury.

love of God is freed from all selfish aims. The enemy of such an ascent is "idle curiosity," and within the monastic precincts *curiositas*, *levitas*, and *singularitas* were to be considered distractions.

Bernard's intellectual asceticism brought him into conflict with established Benedictine monasticism, and his charismatic call for a rejection of pomp and splendor within the monastic church must have seemed threatening to the likes of Cluny and St-Denis. Bernard's attacks on Cluniac monasticism are well-known: he denounced "those abbots who cannot go four leagues from their house without trailing a retinue of 60 horses and sometimes even more in their wake. Will the light only shine if it is in a candelabrum of gold or silver?" But his contemporary reputation probably owed as much to his engagement in political and theological controversy as to his calls for wholesale monastic reform. His political life began in earnest in 1128, when he was chosen to act as secretary to the Synod of Troyes, and immediately managed to have his own draft Rule for the Order of Knights Templar accepted. In 1130, Bernard's advocacy was successful in having Innocent II accepted as pope after a disputed election, and his stock in Rome rose even higher after a former pupil, Eugenius III, was elected pope, again with Bernard as the principal mover.

Theologically, Bernard was no less active. He condemned the teachings of Abelard at the Council of Sens in 1140, took issue with the influential Poitevin scholar Gilbert de la Porrée, and clashed with the Neo-Platonism then beginning to become fashionable in Paris. Bernard's own writings, and notably his *De Consideratione* and *De Diligendo Deo*, are suffused with a poetic mysticism which is without rival in any other twelfth-century work, and assert that God should be loved simply and purely. His commentaries, particularly on the *Song of Songs*, were also extremely influential, and lie behind the later-twelfth-century development of the cult of the Virgin Mary. His greatest disappointment was the Second Crusade. Bernard was responsible for preaching this Crusade, at Vézelay (Burgundy) in 1147, in response to the fall of Edessa. Even Louis VII of France was attracted by the call and agreed to lead the Frankish army, but the venture ended in complete disaster and left the situation worse than it had previously been, bitter news which much preoccupied Bernard in his last years.

Bernward *c.960-1022*
Bishop Feast day November 20

Ordained a priest by Willigis, Archbishop of Mainz, Bernward was appointed to the Imperial Chancellery in 987, and was entrusted with the education of the seven-year-old Emperor Otto III by the regent Theophanu. He traveled extensively with the Imperial court until 993, when he was created Bishop of Hildesheim (Lower Saxony), and it is for his activities in Hildesheim that he is best remembered. A diligent bishop, and founder of the great Benedictine abbey of St. Michael's, Hildesheim, Bernward was among the most significant patrons of art in contemporary Europe, being responsible for the establishment of a bronze foundry in the city. The column and the bronze doors which he donated to his "Temple of the Angel" (St. Michael) testify to the quality of the work Bernward commissioned, and as he was himself a painter and metalworker, must also be regarded as a reflection of his artistic sensibility (his biographer warns that in his own work he does not reach the "peaks of perfection"). He was buried in the western crypt of his own church of St. Michael in 1022, clothed in the habit of a Benedictine monk, and was formally canonized in 1193.

Bridget of Sweden *1303-73*
Founder of the Brigittine order
Feast day July 23

Born into a wealthy Swedish family, Bridget was married to Ulf Godmarson at the age of 14, and had eight children by him. In 1335 she was appointed lady-in-waiting to Queen Blanche of Namur, and as a result of a series of visions, attempted to persuade the Swedish royal family to reform their way of life. In this she was unsuccessful, and from 1341-43 undertook a pilgrimage to Santiago de Compostela (Spain), after which her husband died. Released from marital ties, Bridget founded a monastery at Vadstena (Sweden) in 1346. This was designed for both men and women, the two living in separate enclosures but sharing a single church, as was the case with early-twelfth-century Fontevraud. Again, as at Fontevraud, the men were subordinate to the women, and the abbess acted as head of the entire community.

Bridget traveled to Rome to obtain papal approval for her order in 1349, but follow-

FAR LEFT: Bronze doors (detail), Hildesheim Cathedral. In keeping with his reputation as a metalworker and patron of the arts, Bernward commissioned these bronze doors for his Benedictine abbey of St. Michael at Hildesheim, and witnessed their installation in 1015. The band inscription was probably added by Bishop Godehard, shortly before 1035, when the doors were moved from Bernward's "Temple of the Angel" to be installed in the "Paradise with high towers" (probably the *westwerk*) of the cathedral. Each leaf is 15 feet high and cast in one piece, with eight scenes on the left depicting the Fall of Man from the Creation (top) to the murder of Cain (bottom). The right-hand door chronicles Man's redemption, from the Annunciation (bottom) to a Noli Me Tangere (top).

ing the jubilee of 1350 decided to stay and minister to the poor and sick. The rest of her life, spent either in Rome or on pilgrimage, was impressive in both its austere commitment to the plight of the needy and its political outspokenness. Like **Catherine of Siena**, Bridget called for the papacy to return from Avignon to Rome, and attempted to make peace between warring factions, in this case between English and French armies during the Hundred Years War. Her visions also continued, transcribed and heavily edited by the spiritual advisors appointed by the papacy to oversee her work, whose *Revelations* offer something of a record of her later life. Bridget died in Rome in 1373 and was canonized on October 8, 1391, when her relics were translated to Vadstena.

Catherine of Alexandria
Died c.213?
Virgin and martyr
Feast day November 25

The earliest mention of Catherine is in the ninth century, when her relics were translated to the monastery of Mount Sinai. The inspiration behind the move is uncertain, and the description of her remains carried by the hands of angels probably refers to the Sinai monks, whose profession was often referred to as a call to the angelic life. The earliest surviving accounts of Catherine's life are later still, and appear in the tenth-century *Meonologion Basilianum*

ABOVE: The martyrdom of St. Catherine of Alexandria, fifteenth-century wall painting in SS Peter and Paul, Pickering, Yorks.

LEFT: *St. Catherine Altarpiece* by the Maestro di Sta Cecilia. The altarpiece, probably painted c.1340, shows Catherine flanked by narrative scenes drawn from her life.

RIGHT: *St. Catherine of Alexandria*, Raphael. Majestic early sixteenth-century portrayal of the saint, her wheel simplified and unbroken, her halo reduced to a thin line of gold.

and a near-contemporary life by Symeon Metaphrastes. These place Catherine's death in 312 and concentrate on her martyrdom, though in fact both her existence and translation are highly questionable.

The tenth-century Greek texts maintain that Catherine was born to a noble Christian family in Alexandria, and was of such beauty that the Emperor Maxentius was willing to overlook her refusal to sacrifice to the pagan gods if she would submit to his lecherous desires. Not only did Catherine reject his overtures, claiming she was already the "bride of Christ," but in intellectual debate she conquered the 50 philosophers convened by the Emperor to persuade her of the erroneousness of her beliefs. Indeed, such was the force of her arguments that she converted all 50 to the Christian faith. The philosophers were burned alive, but while in prison, Catherine moved on to convert the Emperor's wife, his General, and two hundred of his troops, which warranted immediate decapitation. Maximian intended to have Catherine broken on a spiked wheel, but by miraculous intervention the wheel was shattered, requiring him to have her beheaded. Milk rather than blood flowed from her severed neck.

The tale proved immensely popular, particularly in the late medieval West, and the *Golden Legend* devotes as much space to Catherine as it does to Mary Magdalen, whose cult she perhaps most resembles. In the late Middle Ages literal depictions emerged of Catherine as a bride of Christ. The term is most often used in medieval exegesis to describe the church, *Ecclesia*, and has complex early Christian roots. The tenth-century accounts of the life of Catherine use the word "bride" loosely, and even the *Golden Legend* speaks quite simply of a vision in which Christ appears to Catherine and says, "Come, my beloved, my spouse, behold the door of heaven is open to thee." A later account expands this into a Mystical Marriage, in which, at the request of the Virgin Mary, an aged anchorite, Adrian, fetches Catherine from Alexandria to a desert church. Here, following her baptism, Adrian celebrates the marriage of Catherine to the Infant Christ. Catherine thereupon faints, and awakens later in Adrian's cell, her only proof of marriage being the wedding ring upon her finger. It is presumably this, or a similar legend which lies behind works such as Hans Memling's 1479 *Mystical Marriage of St. Catherine of Alexandria* in Bruges.

Catherine of Siena
c.1347-80
Dominican tertiary Feast day April 29

Born the youngest of 25 children to Giacomo Benincasa, a dyer in Siena, Catherine's childhood was quite precocious, and to the evident dismay of her parents she experienced religious visions from an early

ABOVE: *The Body of St. Catherine Borne by Angels to Sinai.* Barnardo Luini's fresco of *c.*1520 takes the ninth-century account of the translation of Catherine's relics to Justinian's monastery on Mount Sinai at face value, envisaging a miraculous transportation at the hands of angels. Early medieval writers were much given to comparing the condition of the monk to that of the angel, and the story of Catherine's translation more probably refers to the monks.

age. She resisted all parental pressure to marry during her teens, and in about 1364 became a lay Dominican, or tertiary, though she insisted she wished to live outside any fixed Rule. Catherine was already well known in Siena by this date, and like the once wealthy Sienese merchant and religious penitent, Giovanni Colombini, she formed a *cenacolo*, or lay society, whose Rule, she claimed, came straight from God. Her disciples were all wedded to the idea of charity, penance, and the mystical love of God, ideas which flourished in the climate of violence and uncertainty which scarred Italy in the wake of the Black Death (1348-49). The group included a number of Franciscan and Dominican preachers, one of whom, the Englishman William Flete, had settled to the life of a hermit at Lecceto (Tuscany) in 1362, and was affectionately known as 'the bachelor' on account of his Cambridge degree.

Catherine's personality must have been quite spell-binding, and her religious fervor was so vibrant that members of the *cenacolo* seem to have felt compelled to write short accounts of her life from as early as 1370. One of the best known of these was written in about 1374 by a Florentine disciple, possibly Giannozzo Sacchetti, and concerns one of Catherine's childhood visions, a quite astonishing document which may capture something of the flavor of late fourteenth-century religious experience in Italy.

Raising her eyes toward heaven [Catherine] saw in the air, not very high above the ground, a loggia, rather small and full of light, in which Christ appeared clothed in a pure white garment like a bishop in his cope, with a crozier in his hand; and he smiled at the young girl; and there issued from him, as from the sun, a ray, which was directed at her; and behind Christ [were] several men in white, all saints, among whom appeared SS Peter, Paul and John (*I Miracoli della Beata Caterina*).

This vision is supposed to have happened to Catherine when she was seven, but what is astonishing about such an account is how pictorial it is; one could be describing a painting by Pietro Lorenzetti in Siena Cathedral.

The activities of these lay *cenacoli* came under increasing scrutiny by the Church, as it was felt that their ecstatic Christianity could easily explode into calls for universal penitence and poverty, and that they might begin to resemble the Franciscan Spirituals. Catherine herself was summoned for inter-

rogation before the Dominican Chapter of Sta Maria Novella, Florence, in 1374, and was subsequently assigned a spiritual advisor, the intellectual Dominican Raymond of Capua. Raymond remained with Catherine for the rest of her life, a life which from this date became more and more public. She advocated a Crusade to capture the Holy Land, and tried to persuade the English *condottiere*, Sir John Hawkwood, to lead it. She attempted to make peace between Florence and the papacy, then in Avignon. And she urged Pope Gregory XI to end the so-called 'Babylonian exile' of the papacy in Avignon and return to Rome. Catherine in fact met Gregory in Genoa in 1376, after he had acceded to pressure and was on his way back to Rome, but Gregory's death in 1378 inaugurated the Great Schism, and with rival popes in both cities factionalism be-

ABOVE: *SS Catherine and Bernardino of Siena*. Carlo Crivelli's late fifteenth-century pairing of Catherine of Siena with Bernardino (a Franciscan Strict Observant who spent much of his life in Siena, and died in 1444) was motivated by the increasing devotion felt for both saints within the Franciscan and Dominican orders.

came rife. Catherine supported the Roman candidate, Urban VI, firing off letters to just about every senior churchman in Europe, but it was to no avail, and she died exhausted in Rome on April 29, 1380. Her remains were interred in the church of Sta Maria sopra Minerva in Rome, and in 1461 Catherine was canonized by the Sienese Pope Pius II.

Christina of Markyate
c.1097-c.1160
Virgin Feast day December 5

Christina was the daughter of Autti, an Anglo-Saxon merchant in Huntingdon. According to her contemporary *Vita*, Christina swore a vow of virginity at St. Albans in 1112. This was soon severely tested by Ranulph Flambard, Bishop of Durham, who, having already had children by one of Christina's aunts, visited Huntingdon in 1114 and attempted to seduce Christina. She only escaped by locking Flambard in his room, and spending the night in a pigsty. Flambard revenged himself by arranging her marriage to a local nobleman, Burhtred, and her parents were happy to force through a betrothal. Christina spent most of 1115 in protest and under house arrest, while Robert Bloet, Bishop of Lincoln, first agreed she should not be forced into marriage, and was then bribed into reversing his judgment. Unmoved by the politicking, Christina refused to allow consummation of the marriage, and having been helped to escape, managed to flee to Alfwen the anchoress' refuge at Flamstead (Bedfordshire). In 1118 she moved to nearby Markyate, where Roger the hermit gave her refuge.

This last move scandalized both the royal court and the Church, and Robert Bloet once more intervened, but as Roger's hermitage lay under the jurisdiction of the abbey of St. Albans there was little he could do. The matter was finally resolved in 1122, when Thurstan, Archbishop of York, came to Christina's aid and annulled her marriage, leaving Burhtred, something of an innocent party in all this, free to marry again. Roger the hermit died the following year, and Christina spent the rest of her life at Markyate, refusing both Thurstan's 1130 invitation to take up the position of abbess at St. Clement, York, and the promise of a monastic vocation at Fontevraud. The invitations clearly inspired her and perhaps

concentrated her mind, however, for she did found a convent at Markyate in 1131, and placed it under the protection of Geoffrey, abbot of St. Albans. Christina was a noted seamstress and presented the English Pope Hadrian IV with an embroidered miter she made herself. It also seems likely that she commissioned the *St. Albans Psalter* for private use at Markyate, perhaps between 1123 and 1131.

Christopher *Third century?*
Martyr Feast day July 25

The earliest mention is of a church dedicated to Christopher at Chalcedon (Asia Minor) in 452, and although there are eighth-century legends of Christopher's life in both Greek and Latin, it is obvious that the principal stories only took shape gradually. The most popular, indeed the main late medieval account, is that contained in the *Golden Legend*, according to which the saint was born Reprobus "but after his baptism he was called Christopher, which means Christ-bearer" (*Christophorus* in Greek usually being translated as "one who carries Christ").

The legend maintains that Christopher was a Canaanite "of prodigious size" who sought to serve the most powerful king on earth. The first king he found was fright-

ABOVE: *St. Christopher Carrying Christ*, engraving by Albrecht Dürer. Dürer's realization of the scene shows the hermit who instructed Christopher in the Faith looking on. The shoots at the top of Christopher's staff suggest the flowering palm tree which vindicated Christ's words.

ABOVE RIGHT: *St. Christopher Carrying Christ*, Cosimo Tura, late fifteenth century. Although the iconographical ingredients are the same as in Dürer's engraving, Tura's wiry and metallic sense of form was perhaps intended to evoke a colossal statue, the more familiar late medieval means for representing St. Christopher.

tized, before being arrested for refusing to sacrifice to the gods, possibly during the mid-third-century persecutions of Decius. Two women, Nicaea and Aquilina, were sent into his cell to seduce him, but were instead converted, and his eventual martyrdom consisted of being beaten with iron rods, shot full of arrows, and finally beheaded.

The cult of Christopher enjoyed enormous popularity during the later Middle

BELOW: Thirteenth-century icon invoking Christopher with a dog's head as a protector of travelers. The dog's head was believed to ward off attacks by wild animals.

ened of the Devil and so Christopher went to serve the Devil, but he was astonished to discover that even the Devil quaked at the sight of a cross, and was told "a certain man named Christ was once nailed to a cross, and since then, at the sight of a cross I take fright and flee." He was instructed in the Christian faith by a hermit, and told that to serve Christ he should build a hut along the banks of a river and carry on his back all who wished to cross the river. One night he heard a child's voice imploring him to "carry me across the river." Christopher threw the child on to his shoulders, took up his staff, and waded into the river, but as the water rose the child became heavier and heavier, and he barely made it to the other side. When he set the child down he was told:

Wonder not, Christopher, for not only have you borne the weight of the whole world upon your shoulders, but Him who created and made the world. For I am Christ your King, whom you serve in this work. And as a sign that I tell the truth, when you return to the far bank plant your staff in the earth by your hut, and in the morning you will see it laden with flowers and fruits. And Christopher planted his staff in the earth, and rising in the morning saw it had borne leaves and fruits, like to a palm tree.

His later life seems to have been spent in Samos (Lycia) where he preached and bap-

Ages, when he was not only considered the protector of travelers but was frequently invoked against sudden or accidental death. The tendency to situate late medieval wall paintings or statues of Christopher just inside the main entrance to a church is probably due to the belief that anyone who saw an image of Christopher would not die that day. His patronage of wayfarers also gave rise to the production of the small lead images of the saint beloved of medieval travelers, who carried them as talismans, a tradition perpetuated in modern St. Christopher medallions. The decision of the papacy in 1969 to downgrade the feast to the status of a purely local cult does not seem to have been well received outside the ranks of the clergy; if anything the veneration of St. Christopher, particularly by motorists, seems to be on the increase, hence the popularity of shrines where drivers can come to have their cars blessed on July 25. St-Christophe-le-Jajoulet (Orne, France) being a good example.

Clare *1194-1253*
Virgin and founder of the order of "Poor Clares" Feast day August 11

Born into the noble Offreduccio family in Assisi, Clare must have been aware of the activities of **Francis of Assisi** from an early age, although Thomas of Celano's account of her life places their first meeting in 1208. Moved by his preaching, we are told, she renounced her possessions and joined him at the Portiuncula, only to be sent to the Benedictine convent at Bastia to be trained as a nun. Francis eventually gave her the use of San Damiano in about 1212, which she organized to act as the mother house for a small community of women. This attracted her mother and two of her sisters in addition to a considerable number of other nobly born women. The Rule which Clare drew up was inspired by the *Regula Primitiva* of St. Francis, advocating a life of prayer and absolute poverty. The inhabitants of the early communities were referred to as Minoresses, again inspired by the example of St. Francis, though by the later Middle Ages they were routinely called "Poor Clares."

Success came quickly, and the 1228 *Privilegium Paupertatis* mentions the right of the convents of San Damiano, Perugia, and Florence to maintain a state of poverty and to subsist on alms and beggary alone, thus avoiding, in three houses at least, one of the

problems which beset the Franciscan order during the late thirteenth century (see **Francis**). This papal concession, granted by Gregory IX, suggests other houses were demanding a relaxation of discipline at an early date, but its timing was judicious, for it is unlikely that Clare would have been able to extract it from the papacy in 1230 and it made possible her ideal of an austere contemplative life. That life was spent entirely in Assisi, much of it in prayer, but the various actions she took on behalf of the town suggest a decisive and forceful personality. On two occasions she is recorded as calmly carrying a pyx containing the host to the city walls, when Assisi was under siege from Frederick II Hohenstaufen, and although any causal link with fleeing armies is likely to be exaggeration, the walks are not. Clare was canonized in 1255 by Pope Alexander IV, a mere two years after her death.

ABOVE: *St. Clare.* Eighteenth-century copperplate engraving showing Clare holding the pyx (here a monstrance) with which she saved Assisi from seige.

RIGHT: *St. Clare Mourning St. Francis* by the Master of the St Francis Cycle, Assisi, San Francesco. Wall painting of *c.*1300 which situates Clare's lament outside the church of Sta Chiara, Assisi and contains borrowings from more established types, the Lamentation and Triumphal Entry in particular.

Columba *c.521-97*
Abbot Feast day June 9

Born into the royal Niall clan in Donegal, Columba was trained as a monk by Finnian of Moville. Most of what is known about him is derived from the *Vita Columbae*, an elegant Latin life written by Adamnan, a monk of Iona, around a century after Columba's death. According to this, Columba founded a number of monasteries in Ireland, including Derry and Durrow (where he is known as Columcille), before he decided to become "an exile for Christ" and left Ireland in about 563 with twelve companions. The later traditions offer a variety of motives for this decision: that he became embroiled in a dispute after he was caught furtively copying a fellow-believer's psalter; or intended it as a penance for his involvement in the 561 battle of Cooldrevne; or that he simply wished to work among the heathen Picts. Whatever the reason, he founded a monastery on the island of Iona (Argyll) on land given by the King of Dalraida, from where he managed to convert Bude, king of the Picts. It seems likely that Columba remained responsible for the monasteries he had founded in Ireland throughout his time on Iona, and ruled from there. His death is described in great detail by Adamnan, foreshadowed by many portents which even the abbey horse picked up, and he died in the church on Iona in 597.

Cosmas and Damian
Date unknown
Martyrs Feast day September 26

Cosmas and Damian were martyred at Cyrrhus (Syria) and although nothing is known of the date or circumstances of their death, their cult was well-established in the eastern Mediterranean by the fifth century. A major church was built in their honor in Constantinople, and Pope Felix IV (526-30) adopted a basilica in the forum at Rome, which he had rededicated to SS Cosma e Damiano. Accounts of their life and death, the *Acta* and *Passio*, survive in several versions, but all are relatively late and are considered by scholars to be without historical basis. These maintain that they were twin brothers, skilled in healing the sick, who practiced as physicians but made no charge for their services. Accordingly, they were popularly known as the "silverless ones," and routinely invoked by the sick, who

ABOVE: St. Columba tames a bear, print taken from a bas-relief of 1480 by Giovanni de Midiola. The print illustrates a story of Columba domesticating a wild bear and teaming it with an ox to plow the abbey lands.

LEFT: Cuthbert's pectoral cross. Cross inlaid with garnets and enclosed in filigree gold wire, which was among the personal possessions of Cuthbert which were laid in the shrine at Lindisfarne in 698. Bede describes the cross as old and damaged when placed in the shrine.

would sleep in churches dedicated to the martyrs in the hope of a cure. The *Acta* is concerned with the semi-miraculous recoveries they effected in life, spectacular acts of surgery which include replacing the diseased leg of a black Nubian with a new, healthy, white leg. The *Passio* gives an account of a particularly extended and gruesome martyrdom.

Cuthbert *c.634-87*
Monk and bishop of Lindisfarne
Feast day March 20. Feast of the translation of relics September 2

Although it is probable that Cuthbert was born into an Anglo-Saxon family in Northumbria during the early 630s, the earliest firm date with which he can be associated is 651, when he entered the monastery of Melrose (Borders) as a novice. Eata, abbot of Melrose, had been a pupil of Aidan, the celebrated ex-Iona monk and founder of the monastery of Lindisfarne, and it seems likely that at this date Melrose was run on Celtic lines.

Promoted to the position of guest-master, Cuthbert traveled with Eata to establish a

LEFT: *St. Mark Enthroned between SS Cosmas, Damian, Roche, and Sebastian,* Titian, Venice, Sta Maria della Salute. This altarpiece was commissioned from Titian in late 1510 or 1511 and was intended as an offering in gratitude for the liberation of Venice from a great plague. It was to prove optimistic, for although the plague first struck in 1509 it continued throughout 1512 and recurred with diminishing intensity from 1513-15. It is presumably because it was painted at a time when there seemed little prospect of relief that St. Mark's head is in deep shadow. St. Mark is there as a personification of Venice, and the principal players are Cosmas and Damian (right), surgeons and healers, and Roch and Sebastian (left), intercessors against plague. The altarpiece was originally painted for the church of Santo Spirito in Isola, Venice.

uite & uirtuti ei qfqf legerit inueniet.
'iii Quom adreliqaf qda mirifice fueric ab octi languo
ſanati

monastery at Ripon on estates donated by Alhfrith, but after Alhfrith insisted on Roman usage, both were evicted in favor of Wilfrid. On their return in about 661, Cuthbert was made prior of Melrose. The question of Cuthbert's position during the disputes between the Roman and Celtic Churches over the calculation of the date of Easter is difficult. His earliest biographer maintains he was tonsured in the Roman manner (the familiar bald crown – the Celtic tonsure ran from ear to ear around the back of the skull), but he must have celebrated the Celtic Easter to have been displaced from Ripon by Wilfrid. This issue was referred to a Synod at Streoneshalh (usually identified as Whitby) in 663, where Colman, Bishop of Lindisfarne, presented the Celtic case and Wilfrid argued for Rome. Oswiu, King of Northumbria, came out in favor of Rome, with the result that Colman abandoned his see at Lindisfarne and returned to Iona. Presumably Eata and Cuthbert were among those Celtic-trained monks persuaded by the decision at Streoneshalh, for in 663 Eata was made abbot of the monks of Lindisfarne who had accepted the Roman reckoning, and soon afterward he asked Cuthbert to serve under him as prior.

Despite this acceptance of Roman authority, Cuthbert's life at Lindisfarne seems closer in spirit to Celtic eremitical monasticism than to the strict Benedictine Rule which Wilfrid was introducing at Ripon and Hexham. For a while, he retired to live as a hermit on St. Cuthbert's Isle, relatively close to the monastery, but in 676 he resigned his office of prior in order to withdraw into complete solitude on Inner Farne, an island some six miles south-east of Lindisfarne. It was here, among the birds and seals, that he enjoyed the reveries and contemplative union so eloquently described by Bede in his *Life of St. Cuthbert*. By 684 his reputation for holiness had become so great that Ecgfrith, King of Northumbria, came out to Inner Farne to plead with Cuthbert to accept the bishopric of Hexham. At first Cuthbert was reluctant, but he was eventually persuaded to trade bishoprics with Eata, then in charge of the diocese of Lindisfarne, and on March 26, 685, he was consecrated bishop, with Eata going to Hexham in Cuthbert's stead. The anonymous life written within a few years of Cuthbert's death speaks of him spending these last years traveling about the diocese, preaching, confirming the sheep farmers of the remote Northumbrian hills, and performing miracles. And on March 20, 687, having once more returned to Inner Farne, Cuthbert died.

The news of Cuthbert's death was signaled to the monks at Lindisfarne by lighted torches, and the following morning they carried their beloved bishop to Lindisfarne for burial near the monastic church. The habit of the early Middle Ages was to bury those regarded in their own lifetime as saints in an earth grave, so that the flesh might rot, and then to raise the body in order to wash the bones, wrap them in silks and place them in a shrine. This ceremony was known as "the elevation of the relics" and amounts to a declaration of sainthood. Eadbert, Bishop of Lindisfarne, allowed the elevation of Cuthbert's relics to take place on the eleventh anniversary of his death, in 698. When the body was raised, however, it was found to be incorrupt, a further sign of sainthood, and it was solemnly placed in a shrine on the sanctuary floor of the monastic church. The first miracles were reported within a year of Cuthbert's elevation, and by the time that Bede wrote his magisterial *De*

Vita et Miraculis Sancti Cuthberti in about 720, a considerable pilgrimage to the shrine had taken root.

The destination of this pilgrimage began to change after 875, when persistent Norse raids finally persuaded Bishop Eardulf to take the monks into exile, carrying the relics of St. Cuthbert with them. Their extraordinary odyssey took in Norham-on-Tweed, Ripon, Carlisle and Chester-le-Street, before Cuthbert found eventual peace at Durham in 995 and was enshrined in Bishop Aldhun's White Church. By this time, Cuthbert's shrine had acquired a number of sumptuous donations, given

LEFT: *The Lay of St. Cuthbert*. A diabolical feast is interrupted by St. Cuthbert, here dressed as a pilgrim, who wrestles with a devil over possession of a child.

during the stay at Chester-le-Street. King Athelstan donated an embroidered stole, maniple and girdle, along with a copy of Bede's *Life of St. Cuthbert*, to the community in about 934, while in 945 Edmund, King of Wessex, is recorded as having wrapped the body of St. Cuthbert in two Byzantine cloths "with his own hands."

The bishopric was translated along with the community, and after William Carilef was appointed Bishop of Durham, a second cathedral was begun. Cuthbert was translated to a new shrine behind the high altar in this cathedral on September 4, 1104; although its setting was altered by the construction of the chapel of the nine altars in the mid-thirteenth century, this was the position it occupied for the rest of the Middle Ages. Cuthbert's incorruption was once more verified at the translation, an achievement not to be dismissed in the face of a skeptical Anglo-Norman audience, and his status as the most popular saint of northern England is confirmed in innumerable medieval texts. Even Henry VIII's chantry commissioners were moved by the intactness of Cuthbert's body, and allowed it burial under the medieval shrine site. The body was last exhumed in 1828, when the fragmentary late-seventh-century wooden coffin, textiles, pectoral cross and portable altar were removed and lodged with the cathedral authorities. These are now displayed in Durham Cathedral treasury.

David *Sixth century*
Bishop and patron of Wales
Feast day March 1

Known in Welsh as Dewi or Dafydd, David was adopted as patron of Wales after his canonization by Pope Calixtus II in about 1120. An eighth-century Irish martyrology speaks of Bishop David of Menevia (modern St. David's), and gives March 1 as his feast. Beyond this the early medieval documents make little of David, and although the cult was certainly established in Pembrokeshire by the eighth century, the earliest surviving account of his life was only written c.1090 by Rhygyvarch, a son of the Bishop of St. David's. According to this, David was the son of a Cardigan chieftain, Sant, and was sent to study the Latin scriptures under one Paulinus the Scribe. After his ordination as a priest David founded twelve monasteries, including Crowland, Glastonbury and Menevia (St. David's), which were famous, according to Rhygy-

varch, for their severe discipline and saintly leadership. He then undertook a pilgrimage to Jerusalem, and took the leading role at the Synod of Brevi (Cardiganshire) c.560.

It is on this latter point, David's participation in the Synod of Brevi, that the hagiographer's principal aim becomes clear. Rhygyvarch maintains that David addressed the assembly with such eloquence that "he was made archbishop," and Menevia was thus endowed with metropolitan status. The whole objective of the life is to lend historical support to the claims of the Welsh bishops that they did not owe allegiance to Canterbury. The identification of David as first archbishop of Wales, along with his pilgrimage to Jerusalem, are pure fiction, though that does not mean that all Rhygyvarch's life is unreliable. A council was held at Brevi; David almost certainly did found Menevia; and the early rule seems to have been strict. The title *Aquaticus*, the Waterman, applied to David in a ninth-century document, would indicate that beer, mead or wine were not tolerated within the monastic precincts.

Denis *Died c.251*
Martyr Feast day October 9

According to a passage in Gregory of Tours' *Historiae*, written c.580, Denis was one of the seven "bishops" despatched to Gaul in the mid-third century. On reaching Paris his preaching converted many, and he established a Christian community on an island in the Seine. He fell foul of the Roman authorities, however, and after a short period of imprisonment, was taken to a hill and beheaded, along with his two companions, Eleutherius and Rusticus (the hill subsequently taking the title "Montmartre" or mount of the martyrs.) The bodies of all three martyrs were then fished out of the Seine and buried in the woods to the north of Paris.

A later life of St. Denis alleges that a Christian woman by the name of Catulla built a monument above the graves, which was replaced in about 465 by a basilica, and the complex archaeology of the site can be interpreted as revealing a fifth-century building. What is certain is that by the time Gregory of Tours was writing, a substantial church dedicated to St. Denis had taken shape, and that Aregunde, wife of Clothaire, King of the Franks, was buried there c.580. Gregory even alludes to the shrine arrangements in his *Glory of the Martyrs*:

FAR LEFT: St. Davids Cathedral seen from the east. Little is reliably known of the early history of the site of St. Davids, and the earliest portions of the present fabric date from c.1180. The complex and heterogeneous east end seen here consists of a late twelfth-century presbytery, late thirteenth-century south aisle and early fourteenth-century lady chapel, though all these areas were subsequently refurbished or extended between 1365 and 1523.

LEFT: St. Denis between two angels. Rheims cathedral; north portal of west front. The identification of the central figure as Denis is not without problems, but as he is shown in the robes of a priest and not with the pallium of an archbishop, he is more likely to be Denis than Nicasius, the other major Rheims cult of a martyr, who died through decapitation. The figure dates from c.1230-33 and originally would probably have carried his cranium in his hands. The angel to the left was at one time intended as Gabriel of the Annunciation, but the carrying of a censer indicates that when first carved the figure must have been conceived as the companion to a martyr.

Another man was not afraid to step on the holy tomb [of St. Denis], while he wished to strike with his spear at the gold dove [attached to the tomb]. Because there was a tower on top of the tomb, the man's feet slipped on each side. He crushed his testicles, stabbed himself in the side with his spear, and was found dead. Let no one doubt that this happened by chance, but by the judgment of God.

The church took a further step forward during the reign of Dagobert (628-39), who was lavish in his support for St. Denis, and who may have been responsible for introducing the first community of monks.

Another, very different, story begins to circulate in 830s, promoted by Hilduin,

abbot of St-Denis between 814 and 840. In 827 Hilduin received a Greek manuscript of Dionysius the Areopagite's treatise *On the Celestial Hierarchies* from the Byzantine Emperor Michael II, and with the help of the monks produced a rough Latin translation in the monastic scriptorium. The issues are necessarily complicated, for the author of *On the Celestial Hierarchies* is not the Dionysius who appears in *Acts of the Apostles*, but a fifth-century Syrian monk whom modern scholars refer to as Pseudo-Dionysius. Nevertheless, Hilduin developed the theory that *his* St. Denis was all three figures – the early Christian martyr of Paris, Dionysius the Aeropagite who was converted by St. Paul in Athens, and the author of *On the Celestial Hierarchies*. Hilduin's identification was extremely clever, and a number of details of the life of Denis were rewritten to accommodate it, principally concerned with chronology. Thus after "Dionysius" was converted by Paul, he traveled to Rome and was commissioned by Pope Clement in about 90 AD to evangelize in Gaul. After his martyrdom in Paris, he was not rescued from the Seine but picked up his own head and walked with it to select his place of burial.

With this established, the new legend was broadly accepted, and under Abbot Suger (1122-51) a superb extension of the abbey was begun, which culminated in the consecration of the choir of the "Blessed Martyrs SS Denis, Eleutherius and Rusticus" on June 11, 1144. Suger also made a connection which was to have profound significance for later medieval France, for he established that Denis was lord of the Vexin, and that the King of France was therefore his vassal and should fight in his honor. Furthermore, the emblem of the Vexin was argued to be none other than the Oriflamme, Charlemagne's legendary battle standard, and as this was held in the abbey of St-Denis, French armies owed their allegiance to the saint. Denis had become the patron of France.

Domingo de la Calzada
1019-1109
Hermit Feast day May 12

Born in Viloria de Rioja (Spain), Domingo trained as a monk at the monastery of Valvanera. It seems unlikely that he ever took monastic vows, and in about 1050 he settled to the life of a hermit on the banks of the river Oja. Domingo de la Calzada translates as Dominic of the Causeway, and the title was bestowed after Domingo built a 24-arched bridge to carry the *Camino de Santiago*, the pilgrimage road to Santiago de Compostela in north-west Spain, across the river Oja. Aymery Picaud, writing in the 1130s, maintains he also "built the stretch of road between Nájera and Redecilla del Camino." Domingo subsequently constructed a pilgrim's hospice on the east bank of the river and founded a church on land donated by Alfonso VI of Castile *c.*1098. A significant town grew up alongside the bridge, known in the earlier documents as *Burgo de Santo Domingo*, and by 1232,

taking its title from the cathedral which developed above Domingo's earlier church, Santo Domingo de la Calzada.

Domingo is understandably celebrated as a patron and protector of pilgrims, and a number of late medieval miracles were attributed to his intercession. The most spectacular might be regarded as something of a type-miracle and occurs in several earlier legends, where it is considered the

BELOW: St. Denis hands the oriflamme to Jean Clément, Maréchal de France (Chartres Cathedral). The glass was executed between 1228 and 1231, while Eudes, brother of Jean Clément, was abbot of St-Denis.

work of other saints. Nevertheless, by the late Middle Ages it is firmly attributed to Santo Domingo, and is frequently encountered in the memoirs of fifteenth- and sixteenth-century pilgrims. The form the story most commonly takes alleges that a family of French or German pilgrims were making their way to Santiago, and stopped for the night at an inn at Santo Domingo de la Calzada. The innkeeper's daughter took a fancy to the son, Hugonell, but her advances were spurned. Later that night she hid a silver goblet in Hugonell's scrip, and the following morning she took her revenge by denouncing him as a thief to the local *Corregidor* (magistrate). Hugonell was arrested, found guilty, and hanged, but as his parents were finally preparing to leave, they heard Hugonell whisper that he was alive on the gallows, his feet supported by Santo Domingo. They rushed to tell this to the Corregidor, as he was settling down to dine on a platter of roast cock and hen. The Corregidor retorted that Hugonell was no more alive than his dinner, at which the cock and hen leapt from the plate, sprouted feathers, and crowed the boy's innocence. A live cockerel and hen are still kept in a sixteenth-century coop in the cathedral of Santo Domingo de la Calzada in memory of the miracle.

Dominic *1170-1221*
Founder of the Dominican order
Feast day August 8

Dominic was born at Calaruega (Castile) into an old Castilian family named Guzman, and educated at Palencia. He was appointed a canon of the Augustinian community which served the cathedral of Osma in 1199, rising to the position of prior some two years later. Selected by Diego, Bishop of Osma, to be his companion in preaching against the Cathars (or Albigensians) in Languedoc in either 1203 or 1204, Dominic initially settled in Toulouse, before deciding to work in those rural areas where Catharism had its strongest following. Accordingly he moved to Prouille, where he founded a nunnery in 1206, intending to encourage the formation of a strict Catholic life whose ascetic rigor might compare favorably with that of the Cathar *parfaits*. The murder of the papal legate, Pierre de Castelnau, in 1208 put an end to such subtle methods, and Pope Innocent III's decision to declare an Albigensian Crusade, a vicious campaign which lasted from 1208-18, made

life difficult for those, like Dominic, who saw patient persuasion, rather than mass extermination, as the way to deal with Catharism.

Dominic's great achievement was the foundation of the *Ordo Praedicatorum*, or Friars Preachers (in France also known as Jacobins and in England as Black Friars). This had its origins at Casseneuil, a castle Simon de Montfort made over to Dominic in 1214, where the initial ideas for an order devoted to winning Cathars back to the Church were first developed. Dominic attracted a number of followers, and the community was formally recognized as a religious house by the Bishop of Toulouse in 1215. The decrees of the Fourth Lateran Council of the same year stipulated that new orders should take on an existing Rule, and when Honorius III finally in 1216 issued papal decrees recognizing the community as an order, Dominic was forced to take the Augustinian Rule as his basis. Nonetheless new members were quick to join, and by

FAR LEFT: *St. Dominic* by Fra Angelico. The figure is a detail from a *Mocking of Christ*, painted some time between 1438 and 1446 on the walls of Cell 7 in the reformed Dominican convent of San Marco, Florence.

ABOVE: St. Dominic supervises the burning of heretical texts by the fifteenth-century Castilian artist Pedro Berruguete.

1219 a number of Dominican friaries had been established in Italy, France and Spain.

The first General Chapter was held in Bologna in 1220, and approved the constitution which informed the character of the Dominican order for the whole of the Middle Ages; a body of intellectual priests who might live on a communal basis, but who were principally concerned with work in the community, with teaching, preaching, and bringing the heretical back into the Church. The argumentative rigor of Dominicans became legendary, attracting intellectuals of the caliber of Albertus Magnus and Thomas Aquinas. While their late medieval identification as *Domini Canes*, hounds of God, is unfair when applied to the thirteenth century, it was wholly apposite in the fourteenth, when the order provided the Church with most of the staff for its Inquisition. The great houses were also frequently sited in university cities; it was no coincidence that three of the greatest houses founded in Dominic's lifetime were in Paris, Bologna and Oxford. Dominic himself died in Bologna in 1221, was canonized in 1234, and enshrined in a magnificent tomb commissioned from Nicola Pisano and Arnolfo di Cambio in 1264.

Dunstan *c.910-88*
Monk and archbishop Feast day May 19

Born at Baltonsborough (Somerset) and educated at Glastonbury, Dunstan was related to the royal house of Wessex, and after spending some time at the court of his uncle, Athelm, then Archbishop of Canterbury, he was recruited to serve King Athelstan in Wessex. It seems that Dunstan was unpopular with the other nobles in the king's household, and after contemplating marriage he was persuaded by Aelfheah, Bishop of Winchester, to make his profession as a monk. Aelfheah subsequently ordained Dunstan priest, on the same day as his great friend and contemporary, **Aethelwold**. With the accession of Edmund as king of Wessex in 939, Dunstan was once more brought into government, and some time before the winter of 940 was installed as abbot of Glastonbury. He spent the next 15 years here, launching a program of new building works in 944, and reforming the monastic chapter along strict Benedictine lines.

The major turning-point in Dunstan's life was his banishment by King Eadwy in 955. This seems to have been caused by some

personal slight, and Dunstan chose to spend his exile at the monastery of St. Peter's, Ghent (Belgium), one of the great centers of the European monastic reform movement. Here Dunstan was exposed to monastic thinking on the Continent, and the experience had a profound influence on the subsequent development of the Anglo-Saxon reform movement. Dunstan was recalled by Edgar of Wessex in 957 and invited to take up the bishopric of Worcester, an appointment which was rapidly followed by his promotion to London in 959, and finally to his consecration as Archbishop of Canterbury in 960. In 961 Dunstan also persuaded King Edgar to invite Oswald, who had been trained at the great French abbey of Fleury (St.-Benoît-sur-Loire), to become Bishop of Worcester and Archbishop of York. With Aethelwold created Bishop of Winchester in 963, the scene was set for the monastic reform to begin in earnest.

These three men, with the active encouragement of King Edgar, all of whose lives were so closely interwoven, transformed English religious life during the second half

ABOVE: St. Dunstan, shown in a nineteenth-century engraving. The demon featured top right is here seen escaping from Dunstan's crozier.

of the tenth century. Dunstan was the catalyst, and after the mid-970s he increasingly took a background role. Nevertheless it was his initial reform of Glastonbury which sparked the revival, and his courting of Oswald, Aethelwold and the Continental monks which gave it critical mass. Dunstan was personally responsible for the foundation or refoundation of the abbeys of Athelney, Malmesbury, Bath, Muchelney and Westminster, and the rededication of the old abbey of SS Peter and Paul at Canterbury to St. Augustine. Like Aethelwold he was also a practicing artist, skilled in painting, embroidery and metalwork, and he attached great importance to the role of the artist-monk.

Dunstan's last years were spent almost exclusively among the monks at Christchurch, Canterbury, preoccupied with teaching and supervising the scriptorium. His death, on May 19, 988, occasioned much mourning and his body was buried "in the midst of the choir" in Canterbury Cathedral, the cause, in later years, of a celebrated quarrel with Glastonbury over rights to the possession of Dunstan's relics. Following the completion of the early twelfth-century choir at Canterbury Cathedral, Dunstan's relics were translated. Most unusually, the Romanesque shrine arrangements were described by a monk at Canterbury, Gervase, whose recollection was prompted by the destruction of the choir in 1174. Dunstan was given an altar to contain his relics just to the south of the high altar, and opposite that of St. **Alphege**.

At the eastern horns of the [high] altar were two wooden columns, gracefully ornamented with gold and silver, and sustaining a great beam, the extremities of which rested upon the capitals of two of the pillars [of the main arcade]. This beam, carried across the church above the altar, and decorated with gold, sustained the representations of the Lord, and the images of St. Dunstan and St. Alphege, together with seven chests filled with the relics of divers saints.

Edmund *c.841-69*
King and martyr Feast day November 20

Raised the Christian son of a king of "Saxony", Edmund was chosen as king of the East Angles some time before 865. The principal account of Edmund's martyrdom, the *Passio Sancti Edmundi*, was written at Ramsey Abbey, probably between 985 and 987, by Abbo of Fleury, who maintains he is

LEFT: Most popular representations of St. Dunstan show him as a bishop holding a demon by the nose with a pair of tongs.

BELOW: Miniature of *c.*1170, painted in the scriptorium of Christchurch, Canterbury, and depicting Dunstan amending the Benedictine Rule, from the *Commentary on the Rule of St. Benedict*.

transcribing a tale Edmund's standard-bearer related to St. **Dunstan** (909-88). This is just plausible, but whatever its merits, Abbo was certainly recording an established oral tradition. According to Abbo, Edmund was captured after being defeated in battle by the Norse army of Ingwar in 869. Ingwar bartered his life in exchange for a

half share of the kingdom, but Edmund re-fused to co-operate with a pagan. He was taken to Hellesdon (Norfolk), tied to a tree, and shot full of arrows until he resembled "a thistle." His head was then removed, and was said to have been guarded by a wolf until it could be recovered. He was initially buried nearby, but in about 915 the body was found to be incorrupt and was moved to Bedricsworth (subsequently known as Bury St. Edmunds).

Abbo's narrative does not extend much further than this, but by the late ninth century a considerable cult of St. Edmund had developed, witnessed, for instance, by

the minting of coins bearing the legend *Sc. Eadmund Rex*. King Athelstan founded a community of priests to care for Edmund in 925, and some time before 950 his body was shown to Theodore, Bishop of London. The cult received a further boost in the eleventh century, when Cnut replaced the secular priests with monks, and **Edward the Confessor** added most of west Suffolk to the earlier donations of land. These enormous estates formed the basis of the abbey of Bury St. Edmunds' wealth and prestige during the Middle Ages. The actual display of Edmund's relics took a curious turn, however. Between 1044 and 1065 Edmund's

ABOVE: St. Edmund martyred by the Danes, fifteenth-century wall painting from SS Peter and Paul, Pickering, Yorkshire, showing Edmund on a characteristically late medieval floral background.

RIGHT: Edward the Confessor, detail from the left panel of the *Wilton Diptych* c.1395/99.

coffin was once more opened and his incorruptibility confirmed, but the head was firmly attached to the body, and even a tug-of-war between the abbot and the monks could not separate the two. It was declared that they had been miraculously reunited. There were subsequent openings of the coffin in 1095, when Abbot Baldwin translated Edmund to a new choir, and after a fire in 1198, when Jocelyn of Brakelond remarked that the body seemed too big for its earlier setting, and a new shrine was inaugurated. The latter seems to have been a very grand and unusual affair, with the shrine set high above the ritual choir, and the body said to be visible. Royal saints always attract a political following and Edmund was no exception, being seen in the later Middle Ages as a royal patron of England.

Edward the Confessor
c.1004-66
King Feast day October 13

Edward was the son of the Anglo-Saxon King Ethelred II (the Unready), and his second wife, Emma of Normandy. Following Cnut's accession as sole ruler of England in 1016, Edward was sent with his brother, Alfred, to be educated in the ducal court at Rouen, and only returned to England at the invitation of Cnut's son, Harthacnut, in 1041. Harthacnut nominated Edward his successor, and on his death in 1042 Edward was acclaimed king in London, and crowned in Winchester Cathedral on Easter Sunday, 1043. Historians are divided in their assessments of Edward's reign. Some characterize Edward as an insubstantial figure, fatally weakened in his dealings with Danish and Norman pretenders to the English throne by poor judgment. Others stress his ability to maintain peace in a country which was riven by factional interests, keeping the lid on quarrels between the Anglo-Saxon nobility under Godwine of Wessex, the Danes under Beorn and Swein Estrithson, and Edward's own Norman appointees at court. Edward was certainly forced to make compromises, acquiescing in the deposition of the Norman Robert Champart as Archbishop of Canterbury, after London was disturbed by anti-Norman riots in 1051. Although he did make mistakes, however, his reign was crucial in reopening commercial and intellectual links with Continental Europe.

Edward's reputation for piety is well documented, and turns on his charity to the poor, celibacy (it was believed his marriage to Edith was unconsummated), and personal devotion. He supported Leo IX's call at the 1049 Council of Rheims for the elimination of simony and nepotism in the Church, and around 1050 effectively relaunched Westminster Abbey as a major Benedictine monastery. Edward took a close personal interest in the rebuilding of Westminster, and must have been respon-

sible for the decision to model the church on the abbey of Notre-Dame de Jumièges. As such, Westminster was the first major building in England which might be described as Romanesque. It was also intended to act as his place of burial, and Edward rushed through the consecration of the choir on December 28, 1065, in readiness to receive his body after his death on January 5, 1066.

An anonymous life of Edward, written between 1065 and 1067, attributes several

ABOVE: *Edward and the Pilgrim* (Forthampton Court, Gloucestershire), panel painting of *c.*1370 depicting Edward the Confessor handing a ring to a pilgrim. Similar figures in silver originally stood to either side of the Confessor's thirteenth-century shrine at Westminster.

miracles to him, and maintains he could cure scrofula (known in the Middle Ages as the King's Evil) by the touch of his hand. Nonetheless the cult was slow in taking off, and the motivation behind attempts to have him canonized was wholly political. King Stephen was the first to petition the papacy, in 1138, but Innocent II was unconvinced and demanded that the monks at Westminster collate more information in Edward's support. Henry II (Plantagenet) tried again in 1160, and traded his support for Pope Alexander III against the antipope Victor IV, in return for canonization. This was approved in 1161, and on October 13, 1163, the relics of St. Edward were solemnly translated into a shrine at Westminster Abbey. A second life of Edward was written by the great Cistercian scholar, Ailred of Rievaulx, and as a definite "top-person's saint" the cult began to grow.

Any wider popularity enjoyed by Edward is due to Henry III (1216-72). It was Henry who, "moved by the devotion he had for St. Edward, ordered the church of St. Peter at Westminster to be enlarged" (Matthew Paris: *Chronica Majora*). Matthew Paris' entry is under the year 1245, and it announces the rebuilding of Westminster Abbey, which culminated in a magnificent translation of the relics of St. Edward to a new shrine behind the high altar on October 13, 1267. Henry even commissioned a new version of Ailred of Rievaulx's life from Matthew Paris, and in this form the *Vita Edwardi* was much quoted. The story of Edward and the pilgrim also became popular, and features in a number of surviving paintings, stained glass windows and ceramic tiles. This tells that Edward was importuned by a beggar, in fact St. **John the Evangelist** in disguise, to whom he gave a ring. Some time later St. John revealed himself to two English pilgrims in the Holy Land (said to be from Ludlow in some versions) and handed them the ring, instructing them to restore it to the king on their return, and inform him that within six months they would meet in Paradise. This the pilgrims did, and shortly afterward Edward died.

Elizabeth of Hungary
1207-31
Princess Feast day November 17

Daughter of Andrew II, King of Hungary, Elizabeth was married in 1221 to the Landgrave of Thuringia, Ludwig IV, by whom she

had three children. By all accounts it was an extremely happy marriage, and what was a political match seems to have blossomed into an intense and passionate relationship, mostly spent in the castle at Wartburg. Ludwig's death at Ótranto (Apulia) in 1227, while joining Frederick II's intended Crusade, extinguished this, and it was said that when the news reached Elizabeth her screams filled the castle for days. She left Wartburg that winter, driven out by her brother-in-law, Henry Raspe; the more heart-rending accounts have her thrown into the snow with a baby at her breast.

In 1228 Elizabeth accepted the direction of her confessor, Conrad of Marburg, and took a house at Marburg (Hesse). The few remaining years of her life were spent here working as a Franciscan tertiary, sewing garments for the poor and ministering to the sick in a hospital she constructed close to her home. Her death was certainly hastened by the sadistic treatment she received at the

ABOVE: *St. Elizabeth of Hungary Nursing the Sick* by the seventeenth-century Spanish artist Bartolomé Esteban Murillo. Elizabeth seen in the hospital she founded toward the end of her life in Marburg.

SCA CLARA · SELISABETTA ·

hands of Conrad, who dismissed the household she brought with her from Wartburg, and whose suggested penitential acts included much physical violence. Elizabeth turned down all secular advice to remarry, as well as the invitation of her family to return to Hungary, dying at the age of 24 in 1231. She was canonized in 1235, the same year that the Elisabethskirche at Marburg was begun to enshrine her remains.

Etheldreda *c.630-79*
Virgin and abbess Feast day June 23.
Feast of the translation of relics October 17

Daughter of Anna, king of East Anglia, and traditionally thought to have been born at Exning (Suffolk), Etheldreda was married to Tondberht in about 652 and presented with the Isle of Ely as a dowry, but the marriage remained unconsummated and on Tondberht's death she retired to Ely. A second marriage was forced on her in 660, to Ecgfrith, son of Oswiu, King of Northumbria, but Etheldreda's agreement was conditional on Ecgfrith allowing her to remain a virgin. Ecgfrith's demand, in 672, that he be given full conjugal rights precipitated a bitter dispute, and advised by Wilfrid, then Archbishop of York, Etheldreda abandoned him and took the veil at Coldingham (Lothian). Ecgfrith remarried, and in 673 Etheldreda journeyed south and founded a double monastery at Ely.

Etheldreda spent the last seven years of her life at Ely, organizing the liturgical observances in what rapidly became the pre-eminent monastic community in East Anglia. Like virtually all early Anglo-Saxon foundations, this community was decidedly aristocratic, and Etheldreda was swiftly joined by other members of her family, among them her sister, Sexburga, and great-niece, Walburgh. Her own life at Ely was built around acts of personal renunciation, wearing hair or woollen garments and taking only one meal a day, and her emphasis on the importance of prayer was taken as a model for the whole community. As with Cluny in its early days, the atmosphere seems to have been that of a closely-knit and intimate family. Etheldreda's death in 679 was preceded by the appearance of a tumor on her neck, which a doctor tried and failed to remove, and she was buried in an earth grave in the monastic precincts. When the body was raised some 16 years later, the tumor was found to have healed and her relics to be incorrupt. She was laid in an old

Roman sarcophagus and formally translated to a new resting place by Sexburga on October 17, 695. This became the focus of one of the most important pilgrimages of early medieval England.

Eustace *Second century?*
Martyr Feast day September 20

The earliest accounts of Eustace's life are seventh century, and maintain that Eustace was martyred, along with his wife and two sons, under Emperor Hadrian in about 118. He had been converted to Christianity while hunting in the forests of Guadagnolo (near Palestrina, Lazio), where he experienced a vision of a stag with a crucifix caught in its antlers. This vision was subsequently added to the legend of St. Hubert, and although its origins are obscure, it has points in common with several ancient tribal myths from central Asia. Modern scholars believe that this, and other stories

FAR LEFT: *St. Elizabeth of Hungary and St. Clare*, Simone Martini (Assisi, lower church of San Francesco). The arrangement of saints at dado level in the chapel of St. Martin is a roll-call of those favored within the Franciscan order. Elizabeth (right) is here paired with Clare.

ABOVE: St. Etheldreda, from the *Benedictional of St. Aethelwold*. Aethelwold reformed the monastery of Ely during the 970s, and an indication of the esteem in which he held its church and relics is his inclusion of Etheldreda in the *Benedictional* of 971-84.

of St. Eustace, are not the result of the simple conferment of legends on an otherwise historical martyr, but that the entire cult was invented. It proved to be a popular legend, and a number of churches were dedicated to the cult, including an eighth-century basilica in Rome, Sant'Eustorgio, and the eleventh-century church of Sant'-Eustorgio at Milan. Some relics even surfaced in twelfth-century Paris, doubtless contributing to the growth of the cult in medieval France, and it was here that St. Eustace enjoyed his greatest following. The finest witness to this is perhaps the superlative window recounting his life, given by the drapers and furriers to Chartres Cathedral (north nave aisle).

Francis of Assisi *1181-1226*
Founder of the Franciscan order
Feast day October 4

Born to an Umbrian cloth merchant, Pietro Bernadone, and his Provençal wife Pica, both then settled in Assisi, Francis' youth was spent working in the family business, during which time he seems to have gained a reputation for high living. The border war of 1202-03 between Assisi and Perugia put paid to this; Francis was captured and held prisoner for the best part of a year. His return to Assisi coincided with a serious illness, and it would appear to be this illness, or rather the long periods of introspection which accompanied it, which prompted his decision to devote his life to prayer and the needs of the poor. Shortly afterwards, while lying prostrate before a crucifix in the tiny church of San Damiano (just outside the walls of Assisi) he heard a voice say: "Francis, go and repair my house, which as you see is falling into ruin."

Most commentators see this moment as marking the beginning of Francis' mission. In order to restore San Damiano, Francis sold a bale of his father's cloth, provoking a protracted dispute which culminated in his renouncing his inheritance, a significant act which was to play a vital role in later accounts of his life, where it is known as the renunciation of worldly goods. He then spent several years traveling alone as a mendicant preacher, eventually attracting seven disciples, with whom he established a community at the Portiuncula, some three miles south of Assisi. It was here, *c.*1209, that Francis composed the first, simple Rule to regulate the life of himself and his disciples, the *Regula Primitiva*, which was approved by Pope Innocent III in 1210. The Rule was part-monastic, part-apostolic, requiring the brethren to spread the gospel through preaching and journeying, while stressing the importance of obedience to Church authority and poverty. Adopting the name *Fratres Minores* (friars minor, literally lesser brothers), they enthusiastically took to the roads, organizing huge preaching tours, after each of which they would return to the Portiuncula to lead a life of prayer and manual labor, supplemented, if necessary, by begging.

Expansion was rapid and a second convent was soon established in Bologna, while a local noblewoman, **Clare**, founded a

ABOVE: The Vision of St. Eustace (Paris, Cathedral of Notre-Dame). A number of important stained glass windows were devoted to St. Eustace in northern France during the thirteenth century, the period when the cult enjoyed its greatest following. The cathedrals of Chartres, Sens, Tours and Paris were among those to play such a role in propagating the life of the saint.

BELOW LEFT: *St. Francis in Meditation*, by the seventeenth-century Spanish artist Francisco de Zurbarán.

RIGHT: *The Vision of St. Eustace*, woodcut, 1501, by Albrecht Dürer. At some point during the fourteenth century, the story of the conversion of St. Eustace while out hunting on Good Friday was added to the life of St. Hubert, an eighth-century Bishop of Maastricht.

parallel community for women in 1212, initially based at San Damiano. Francis also began to formulate a mission to convert the Muslims. In 1214 he traveled across southern France and Spain, intending to reach north Africa, but was forced to return through illness. And in 1219, accompanied by eleven of the brethren and an army of Crusaders under Gautier de Brienne, he sailed from Ancona for Acre, becoming involved in the siege and capture of Damietta. He eventually reached Egypt, where he was granted an audience with Sultan Malek al-Kamel but, despite the success of his trial of faith by fire, the Sultan did not convert, and Francis returned to Italy dispirited by his lack of success and shattered by the rapacity of the Christian Crusaders.

Once home he was confronted by another, very different, problem. The order had been growing rapidly before he left, and numbered 5000 by 1220, each friar attached to a local foundation. Lacking a formal administrative structure, with no novitiate or means of governing admissions, the Friars Minor faced serious questions as to how a simple Rule might be applied to a now complex organization. Francis argued that he lacked the administrative skills needed to lead the order, and resigned his office of Minister-General at the General Chapter of 1220 in favor of Elias of Cortona. Then, in 1221, he drew up another Rule, the *Regula Prima*, which reiterated the commitment of the *Regula Primitiva*, to poverty, humility and evangelical zeal, but which was amended at the insistence of the General Chapter, before finally being approved by Pope Honorius III on November 29, 1223, after which it became known as the *Regula Bullata*. A 'Protector' of the order was also appointed by the papacy, the first of whom, Ugolino da Ostia, was himself to become pope in 1227, taking the title Gregory IX.

It is to the last years of his life that many of the most famous stories of France belong: the miracle of the crib at Greccio; the death of the knight of Celano; the miracle of the spring; the visit to Clare, when he wrote the *Canticle of the Sun*; and the gift of the stigmata on Monte La Verna (the last two in 1224). The scars of the stigmata, corresponding to the five wounds on the body of the crucified Christ, are thought to be responsible for the extreme pain and ill-health he suffered toward the very end of his life, and after two years of agony he died at the Portiuncula on October 3, 1226.

Both the cult of Francis and the Franciscan order developed in exceptional ways after his death. Initially buried in the church of San Giorgio at Assisi, Francis was canonized by Gregory IX in 1228, and translated to the crypt of the new church of San Francesco at Assisi in 1230. In the meantime Gregory IX also had a life of St. Francis commissioned from Thomas of Celano, the so-called *Vita Prima*. Francis' own writings, however, particularly the *Testament* and the *Canticle of the Sun*, began to be disputed within the order, and two strands of opinion seem to have crystallized quite quickly. In 1230 Gregory IX declared that the *Testament* was not universally binding on the order and had the *Vita Prima* rewritten. By then the strands of opinion had hardened into factions and Gregory's actions helped to polarize them. Those who supported Gregory argued that the rapid spread of the order and the need for settled houses made the prohibition on ownership of property, either personal or corporate, unworkable; they favored a relaxed and pragmatic interpretation of the Rule, and became known as Conventuals. Those who opposed Gregory and insisted on the strict interpretation of the letter of the rule were known as Strict Observants, subsequently becoming more popularly known as the Spirituals.

The dispute became uncommonly bitter, particularly during the Minister-Generalship of Bonaventure (1257-74). One of Bonaventure's first acts was to negotiate with the papacy the doctrine of *usus simplex*, whereby all Franciscan property was held by the Church, and the order simply enjoyed 'use' of it. More radically, at the 1266 General Chapter in Paris, Bonaventure was commissioned to write a new life of St. Francis, the *Legenda Maior*, and all early accounts of the life of the saint were ordered to be destroyed. One result of this blatant censorship was the growth of secondary legends, notably those contained in the *Little Flowers of St. Francis*, but although scholars have recovered sections of an early account by Friar Leo, much of the detail of Francis' life has been lost. The famous cycle of paintings of the *Life of St. Francis* in the upper church of San Francesco at Assisi is explicitly based on the *Legenda Maior*, and as this achieved virtual "canonical" status, the version it put forward was followed in most of the later pictorial accounts. The Spirituals left the order between 1317 and 1321.

PREVIOUS PAGES: *The Funeral of St. Francis*, by Domenico Ghirlandaio (Florence, Sta Trinità). Ghirlandaio's fresco of 1485 takes a number of motifs from the representation of the same scene in the upper church of San Francesco at Assisi, *c.*1300. Borrowings include the presence of a nobleman dressed in red verifying the stigmata, the positioning of Francis on a central bier, the mingling of Franciscans, secular clergy and laity, and the chanting of the obsequies. The locale has changed, however, and rather than situating the funeral beneath a simple rood beam, Ghirlandaio has constructed an elaborate ecclesiastical temple.

FAR LEFT: *St. Francis Preaching to the Birds*, sixteenth-century woodcut. Perhaps the most famous of all those stories of St. Francis which emphasize his empathy with the natural world, a story which features in both the *Little Flowers of St. Francis* and Bonaventure's *Legenda Maior*.

Frideswide *c.680-727*

Virgin and abbess Feast day October 19.
Feast of the translation of relics
February 12

Recent research has established that Frideswide was the daughter of the Mercian sub-king Dida of Eynsham, who made her the founding abbess of his monastery at Oxford. The standard medieval account of her life is that recorded, though not composed, by the early twelfth-century chronicler William of Malmesbury. This makes much of an attempted seduction of Frideswide by Aethelbald of Mercia, who was temporarily blinded after Frideswide had fled into the forests near Binsey, and whose sight was restored as a result of her intercession. Frideswide died at her monastery in Oxford, and although the church, with its burden of documents and charters, was destroyed in 1002, there is little doubt that her relics occupied a shrine by the eleventh century at latest. This church is mentioned as bearing a dedication to St. Frideswide before the Conquest, although the nuns of Frideswide's monastery had by this date given way to secular canons.

An early-twelfth-century reform reconstituted the church as a house of Augustinian canons, and the cult of St. Frideswide gained in popularity as the population of Oxford began to grow. Two translations, in 1180 and 1289, attest to this popularity, each shrine bigger, better, and more accessible than the previous, and by 1434 her feast was celebrated as that of the patron of Oxford University, a position she still occupies. The church was eventually annexed by Cardinal Wolsey, its precincts acting as the site for his new Cardinal College (now Christ Church College), and the shrine was despoiled by Henry VII's chantry commissioners in 1538. Nonetheless in 1546 this church was raised to the rank of cathedral, under the new title of Christ Church, where a few fragments of St. Frideswide's late thirteenth-century shrine base survive to this day.

George *Died c.304*

Martyr Feast day April 23

Practically nothing is known of George's life, but the cult is early and his feast is mentioned in the mid-fifth-century *Hieronymianum*. It is possible that the *Acta* of St. George revised at the request of Pope Gelasius in 494, and which formed part of the proceedings of a council in Rome, was

LEFT: St. Frideswide (Hereford Cathedral), mid-nineteenth century representation in stained glass.

RIGHT: *St. George and the Dragon*, French manuscript illustration. The obvious parallels between the story of George triumphing over the dragon (thus championing the king's daughter) and the ethics of late medieval tournaments, led artists to recompose the scene as if it were a tourney. In this mid-fifteenth century French miniature, the action is set on a gentle hill above the town, an audience gathers upon the parapet walls amidst hanging banners, and the king's daughter stands above a rocky eminence to witness the action.

fourth century, but the earliest Latin texts which now survive are ninth century. These undoubtedly derive from a Greek original. Gelasius' interest was inspired by the proliferation of miracle stories accruing to St. George, and it seems he sought to play down the more spectacular tales of George's resurrection while under torture. Accordingly an expurgated reading of the life was produced, known to scholars as the *Canonical Version*, while the fuller account, known as the *Apocryphal Version*, continued to circulate in the East. A number of recensions, part-way between the two, also surfaced in the West during the tenth and eleventh centuries. All of these agree that George was a soldier martyred at Diospolis (now Lydda, Palestine) in the reign of the Emperor Diocletian, perhaps during the Great Persecution of 304-305.

The descriptions of George's death are

indeed spectacular, even when reduced to theological respectability, and the story given here is closer to the *Canonical* than the *Apocryphal* version. Having refused to take part in a sacrifice to Apollo, George was arrested by Dacian, Roman governor of Diospolis, and tied to a cross, where his skin was scraped with iron combs. He was then nailed and chained to a wooden board and thrown into prison, where he spent the night comforted by Christ and a choir of angels. The following day Dacian again bade him sacrifice to Apollo, and on hearing his refusal, had a magician mix a strong poison for George to drink. George made the sign of the cross over the poison and drank first one and then a second cup, remaining upright throughout. Seeing his initiative overcome by a power greater than his own, the magician converted, and was instantly executed by Dacian. Next Dacian had George scoured between two wheels,

but the wheels were miraculously broken. He then had him sawn in two, and this did kill George, but he was resurrected by divine intervention and made whole. He was then thrown into a cauldron of molten lead, where he remained at peace and unharmed. By now quite exasperated, Dacian tried a new ploy and flattered George into agreeing to worship in the temple of Apollo, but George called upon God to destroy the temple. The following morning Dacian had him dragged naked through the streets and finally beheaded. With this done, a great fire descended from the skies and destroyed Dacian and his court.

In none of these early medieval accounts is there any mention of George and the dragon. This most famous of his deeds only seems to have been added to the hagiographies in the wake of the First Crusade (1096-99). The *Gesta Francorum* claims that a vision of SS George and Demetrius

ABOVE: *St. George and the Dragon*, Vittore Carpaccio. St. George became the patron not only of England, but also of Catalonia, Genoa and Dalmatia, hence Carpaccio's superb portrayal of 1502-8 in the Scuola di San Giorgio, the Venetian headquarters of the Confraternity of Dalmatians.

FAR RIGHT: *St. George and the Dragon*, early twentieth-century relief from Budapest.

appeared to the Crusaders during the Siege of Antioch (1098) and gave rise to a popular belief that George was the special patron of crusaders. Richard Coeur-de-Lion took matters a stage further and placed his own army under the protection of St. George in 1189. The legend of the dragon first appears between these two dates, and was further refined before it achieved quasi-canonical status in the *Golden Legend*, compiled some time between *c.*1255 and *c.*1273. According to this, George was a Cappadocian "knight" who was travelling across north Africa. At Silene (Libya) he encountered a people terrorized by a local dragon, whose lair was by a lake just outside the city. The dragon could only be pacified by a daily sacrifice and at first had been happy to accept two sheep, but as these became depleted, a youth or maiden, chosen by lot, was offered instead. After many young had been devoured, the lot fell upon the king's

daughter and, despite the king's despairing offer to trade his fortune for a substitute, the people of Silene insisted the sacrifice should go ahead, "according to the king's word that none are to be exempt." George arrive as the king's daughter, dressed as a bride, was being led to the dragon. On learning why she was there, he charged, pierced the dragon's side, and tied the princess' girdle about its neck. The dragon was then led "like a little dog on a leash" into the city and killed.

In an age anxious to equate chivalric codes with soldiering, George became understandably popular, and was enthusiastically embraced in Catalonia, Portugal, Venice and Crete. His adoption as the patron of England also seems to have arisen out of this connection. Edward III was particularly attached to the cult, and placed his new Order of the Garter under the patronage of St. George in 1347. The arms of St. George, a red cross on a white ground, first appear on English surcoats and shields at a roughly similar date.

Germanus of Auxerre
c.380-448
Bishop Feast day July 31

A brilliant fifth-century churchman, Germanus was born to an aristocratic Gallo-Roman family in Auxerre and trained as a lawyer in Rome. His legal advocacy won him a high reputation and under the Emperor Honorius (395-423) he was appointed governor of Armorica, conventionally used to describe Brittany, although the areas over which Germanus wielded authority coincide more with what is now northern Burgundy. Despite his protestations of unsuitability, he was elected Bishop of Auxerre on the death of Amator in 418, and in 429 was sent to Britain to help in combatting the Pelagian heresy (a system which holds that the individual is responsible for the first steps toward salvation through his or her own efforts, and named after the late fourth-century British theologian, Pelagius), and successfully refuted the heretics at Verulamium (St. Albans). He returned a second time in 447 when, it is alleged, he masterminded a British victory in battle against an alliance of Picts and Saxons, teaching the Britons to use "Alleluia" as a war-cry (the "Alleluia Victory").

The following year he journeyed to Ravenna where, before Galla Placidia,

mother of Honorius and effective ruler of Ravenna, and Emperor Valentinian III, he represented the cause of the Bretons against the imperial administrators of north-western Gaul. It was also here, on July 31, 448, that he died, his body being returned by devoted women followers to Auxerre for burial in a small oratory above the east bank of the river Yonne. This formed the nucleus of an important monastery founded by Clothilde in the early sixth century, and subsequently magnificently extended under the Carolingian emperor Charles the Bald, when the crypt acted as the focus for a substantial medieval pilgrimage to the shrine.

ABOVE: *St. George and the Dragon* by the nineteenth-century British artist Sir Edward Poynter.

Gervase and Protase
Date unknown
Martyrs Feast day June 19

Nothing is known of the lives of Gervase and Protase, though the broadly contemporary accounts of both Paulinus and **Augustine of Hippo** agree on the discovery of their relics. This came about in 386, after **Ambrose** experienced what he described as a "presentiment" while at prayer in the church of SS Nabor and Felix in Milan. He ordered the pavement to be excavated and two decapitated skeletons were discovered, which he had translated to his own church (the present Sant'Ambrogio, Milan). A later tradition maintains that Gervase and Protase were the twin sons of St. Vitalis and were martyred in the late second century, while the *Golden Legend* finds Nero responsible for their death. What is beyond doubt is that the relics proved miraculous, and even Augustine of Hippo, in his *De Civitate Dei*, speaks of witnessing a blind man recover his sight at the tomb.

It was undoubtedly this proven miracle-working power which lies behind the

BELOW LEFT: *SS Gervase and Protase*, engraving of 1880. Gervase and Protase being led to their martyrdom outside the city walls of Milan.

OVERLEAF ABOVE: SS Gervase and Protase construct a chapel. Scene from a tapestry cycle of the lives of the saints installed in Le Mans Cathedral in 1510. The cathedral was initially dedicated to SS Gervase and Protase in the early fourth century.

OVERLEAF BELOW: The martyrdom and burial of SS Gervase and Protase.

spread of the cult, and portions of the saints, along with strips of cloth which had touched their bones, began to circulate in fifth-century Europe. The cult was particularly popular in late Roman Gaul, and the cathedrals of Le Mans, Sées (Normandy), and Soissons all took dedications to Gervase and Protase. The relics of Ambrose were eventually joined with those of the twin martyrs in a porphyry sarcophagus, and placed beneath a magnificent golden altar by Archbishop Angilbertus, some time between 843 and 859. This, the *Paliotto*, still

stands in the choir of Sant'Ambrogio, Milan, the sole Carolingian golden altar to survive in Europe and a sumptuous reminder of the aesthetics of early medieval reliquary cults.

Giles *Seventh century?*
Hermit Feast day September 1

In medieval Latin texts Giles is referred to as Aegidius, founder of the monastery which bears his name, St-Gilles (Provence). A tenth-century history, the *Vita Sancti Aegidii*, is the principal source for his life, but

RIGHT: *The Mass of St. Giles* (Master of the Mass of St Giles *c*.1500). Given Giles' credentials as a protector of France, an annual mass was held in his honor at the abbey of St-Denis.

largely consists of transfusions from the lives of other saints. This maintains that Giles was an Athenian who retired to live as a hermit near Nîmes. One day, while out hunting, the Visigothic king Wamba shot and crippled Giles with an arrow, intending to bag a hind which had leapt to take refuge in Giles' lap. Impressed by his piety and tranquillity, Wamba gave Giles a grant of land on which to found a monastery. A second, much repeated, tale recounts the visit of an emperor (subsequently identified as Charlemagne), anxious for Giles to pray for his forgiveness. Although the Emperor refused to divulge the nature of his sin, Giles saw it written down by an angel and as he prayed the sentence faded away. The stories are enchanting early medieval stereotypes, and associate Giles with saints and rulers regardless of chronology, but they occasionally chime with legal documents; a surviving papal bull does recount the foundation of a monastery by Wamba on behalf of Giles, to which Pope Benedict II (684-85) granted a charter.

The cult was immensely popular between the tenth and fifteenth centuries, particularly among cripples, lepers and beggars. The dedication of St. Giles, Cripplegate (London), recalls the former connection, while the creation of hospitals in honor of St. Giles (over 60 are known in medieval Europe) reflects the concern for lepers and the poor.

Gregory the Great
c.540-604
Pope Feast day September 3

Born to a senatorial family in Rome, Gregory was appointed prefect in 573, at the same time selling his personal estates for the relief of the poor. Gregory was responsible for founding a number of monasteries in Sicily and one, San Andrea, in Rome, and it was in the latter that he became a monk in about 575. His monastic experience was short-lived; he became, first, one of the deacons of Rome, and shortly afterward papal representative in Constantinople. He returned from the East around 585 and became abbot at San Andrea, but was elected pope in 590 and once more forced out of the monastic life.

Gregory's 14-year papacy is considered by scholars to be the most influential of the early Middle Ages. His sidestepping of the claims of the Byzantine Exarchs of Ravenna

in order to negotiate treaties with the Longobards of northern Italy in 592 effectively marks the break between Rome and Constantinople, while his decision to send **Augustine** on a mission of conversion to England in 596 was responsible for the organization of the Church in Britain along Roman lines. His support for monasticism was crucial for the development of the Church in the Latin West, as was his reform of the administration of ecclesiastical estates. To this formidable list should be added his achievement in codifying the responsibilities of a bishop, crystallized in his *Pastoral Care* (c.591); the impact of his defence of the institution of pictorial images in churches; and his contribution to the development of the Roman liturgy. The latter has become the subject of much controversy, for although a number of texts enshrined in the *Gregorian Sacramentary* are

ABOVE: St. Gregory dictates his *Pastoral Letters* to a scribe, twelfth-century manuscript illumination. Gregory, under the direct inspiration of the Holy Spirit (here seen as a dove whispering into his ear), is glimpsed by his scribe from behind the curtain.

Gregory's, the work as a whole is a later anthology of pieces from a number of hands. Equally, the term "Gregorian Chant" as a description of liturgical plainsong may overstate Gregory's personal involvement, but his reorganization of the Roman school of chant was the catalyst for its adoption throughout the western Church.

Guthlac *c.673-714*
Hermit Feast day April 11

Born into a noble Mercian family, Guthlac trained as a soldier. According to Felix, whose Latin life of Guthlac was probably written shortly after his death, and certainly before 749, Guthlac served in the Mercian army for nine years. Late seventh-century Mercian history is otherwise little recorded, and for most of this period it is likely that Guthlac was involving in raiding parties, laying waste his enemies' lands with fire and the sword, to paraphrase Felix. Disillusioned, he entered the double monastery of Repton (Derbyshire) in about 697, then under the rule of the abbess Aelfrith. It seems his refusal to drink alcohol made him unpopular with the monks, and although he was later reconciled with the community, he decided after about four

ABOVE AND BELOW: Scenes from the life of Guthlac. The four roundels represent Guthlac receiving the tonsure; sailing to Crowland; building an oratory; visited by King Aethelbald. The Harley roll from which these scenes are taken probably dates from 1196, and may be a *vidimus*, or compositional sketch, for stained glass.

years to leave the precincts and adopt the life of a hermit.

Guthlac established a retreat for himself on an island in the Fens at Crowland (Lincolnshire), a solitude which acted as his home for the rest of his life. A good number of the stories which Felix associated with Guthlac's life at Crowland were borrowed from the lives of the Desert Fathers, and in particular from a fourth-century life of St. Anthony of Egypt. Accordingly, Guthlac was a frequent object of attack from spiritual foes, endlessly hounded, bitten and tempted by demons. He was also harried by the *emigré* Britons who had been driven into the Fens by earlier German invaders. Most representations of Guthlac center on these conflicts, and the cult was very much that of the tormented hermit. Its popularity began to grow in the ninth century, and Thurketyl's rebuilding of a monastic church destroyed during the Danish raids provided a considerable boost. This was once more destroyed in 1091, but the various Romanesque and Gothic rebuildings eventually left Crowland one of the most important Benedictine abbeys to grace medieval East Anglia.

Hildegard of Bingen
1098-1179
Poet, musician, and nun
Feast day September 17

Hildegard was born into the noble family of Hildebert of Gut Bermesheim (Rheinhessen) and educated at the local convent of Disibodenberg. She made her profession as a nun at Disibodenberg in 1113, and on the death of her mentor and abbess, Jutta of Spanheim, in 1136, was elected *magistra* (superior). Following her election the community began to grow, and rather than expand the existing precincts, Hildegard founded a new convent at Rupertsberg, near Bingen, whose construction she personally supervised. The rest of an extraordinarily long and active life was spent here, organizing the conventual liturgy, composing hymns, poetry and academic theses, and engaging in a wide-ranging correspondence with the likes of Henry II of England, Frederick Barbarossa and Pope Eugenius III.

Hildegard is perhaps best known for her visions and her music. She experienced the former throughout her life, and was persuaded in about 1141 to begin recording

them in a manuscript entitled *Scivias* (or *Sciens Vias* – know the way). Two other visionary works followed, the *Liber Vitae Divinorum* and *De Operatione Dei*. In addition to these, Hildegard wrote treatises on medicine, natural history and the Benedictine Rule. Her music has enjoyed a revival over the last decade, and she is now most celebrated as one of the foremost composers of the twelfth century. Of the 70 or so vocal compositions which survive, the most ambitious is perhaps the *Ordo Virtutum*. This is thought to have been created to celebrate the consecration of the convent of Rupertsberg in 1152, and takes the form of a series of musical confrontations between 16 Virtues and the Devil. The parts of the Virtues were sung by the nuns, the female voices embodying the hope and mercy of the New Testament, while the male parts

ABOVE: St. Hildegard inspired by heavenly fire while the monk, Volmar, transcribes her visions. Miniature of c.1165 from the *Rupertsberger Codex*.

RIGHT: *Christ in Majesty*, apse painting, Berzé-la-Ville. Some time between 1093 and 1109 Hugh of Cluny authorized the restoration of the chapel of Berzé-la-Ville to act as his private retreat, and may well have commissioned the apse painting.

are restricted to the prophets and patriarchs of the Old Testament, the outworn strictures of the old law. Not only does this reverse standard practice in twelfth-century musical drama, but the only other role for the male voice is the part of the Devil.

Hildegard died at the age of 80 and was buried at Rupertsberg, but despite attempts on the part of the nuns to have her canonized, formal recognition was withheld. Her name appears in a fifteenth-century revision of the *Roman Martyrology*, however, and the cult became popular in late medieval Germany.

Hugh of Cluny *1024-1109*
Abbot Feast day April 29

Son of the count of Sémur-en-Brionnais, Hugh was raised in the household of an older relative, Hugh, Bishop of Auxerre. He entered the monastery of Cluny (Burgundy), was ordained a priest, and appointed prior by Odilo in 1048. On Odilo's death in 1049 he was elected abbot of Cluny, a position he was to occupy for the next 60 years. With such a position came responsibility, and it is primarily to Hugh that Cluny owes its medieval prestige. By the date of Hugh's election Cluny had brought a number of important monasteries under its direct control, including La Madeleine at Vézelay. The justification for this was that it would allow them to enjoy Cluny's exemption from lay or episcopal control, and ensure strict obedience to the ideals of reformed Benedictine monasticism. Hugh pushed this principle to its limits, and added such venerable institutions as Moissac, St. Bertin, St-Germain-d'Auxerre and Beaulieu to the greater congregation of Cluny, as well as encouraging the foundation of major new monasteries at La Charité-sur-Loire, Poitiers and Lewes (Sussex).

The success of this policy can be seen in the 1450 houses listed as monastic dependencies of Cluny in the late Middle Ages, nearly all of them brought under Cluniac control by Hugh. And with an ex-monk of Cluny elected Pope Urban II in 1088, Hugh's position as the leading monastic reformer in Europe was assured. It was in this same year, 1088, that work began on a new church at Cluny, which, when completed in about 1130, was the largest in Latin Europe. Urban II's consecration of the high altar of this church on October 25, 1095, was accompanied by his description of Cluny as *Lux Mundi*, the light of the world, and in addi-

tion to granting Cluny the status of monastic order in its own right, Urban conferred on Hugh the right to wear pontifical vestments at Mass – purple gloves, a jeweled miter and gold-embroidered slippers.

All this might suggest that Hugh harbored vain ambitions for his monastery, and this was certainly the way **Bernard of Clairvaux** perceived Cluny a generation after Hugh's death, but one should not underestimate the integrity or discipline with which Hugh conducted his life. His contribution to the ecclesiastical reform of eleventh-century Europe was immense, and as a confidant of Pope Leo IX, he joined the papacy in condemning the teaching of Berengar of Tours at the Easter Synod of Rome in 1050. Hugh also assisted at every major Roman council of the late eleventh century and, as a keen supporter of Hildebrand's Gregorian reform movement, acted as broker in the dispute between Pope Gregory VII and the Emperor Henry IV.

Hugh of Lincoln
c.1135-1200
Carthusian monk and bishop
Feast day November 17

Born to a noble family at Avalon (near Grenoble in the French Dauphiné), Hugh was initially trained as an Augustinian canon, but decided to adopt a more austere religious life while in his early twenties, and became a monk at the great Carthusian monastery of the Grande Chartreuse in about 1160. His reputation as an administrator brought him to the attention of Henry II of England, who persuaded Hugh to accept the position of prior at his recently founded Charterhouse of Witham (Somerset). Hugh attached certain conditions to his appointment: that Henry recompense any local inhabitants who had been displaced to make way for the monastic precincts, and equip the monastery with a suitable library. Further promotion came in 1186, when Henry nominated him Bishop of Lincoln, a position he was again reluctant to accept. Hugh was only eventually installed after his insistence on a free election had been accommodated, owing to considerable pressure from the prior of the Grande Chartreuse.

Hugh's term as Bishop of Lincoln coincided with the building of a new cathedral choir (the present St. Hugh's Choir), a project on which his biographers maintain he

LEFT: These choir stalls were installed in 1558 on the south side of the lay brothers' choir in the Carthusian monastery at Miraflores, just above Burgos (Spain). In keeping with the traditions of the order, they celebrate prominent Carthusian saints. St Hugh of Lincoln can be seen fourth from the left, holding the infant Christ in a chalice.

"worked with his own hands." He was immensely productive in other areas too, presiding at a number of important synods and court cases. Hugh took an independent line in his relations with the secular authority. He protested the rights of the peasantry against royal foresters, rejected most court nominations to ecclesiastical appointments, and physically intervened to protect Jews at risk from rioting mobs in Lincoln and Northampton. His reputation as a champion of the oppressed received a further boost from his refusal, along with Herbert Poor, Bishop of Sarum, to provide Richard I with knights for service overseas at the 1197 Council of Oxford, an event with enormous significance for future political history.

Hugh's program of visitations to the outlying areas of his vast diocese was tireless, and after each itinerary he would return to Lincoln, or his manor at Stow (Lincolnshire), to tend his pets. His earliest biographer, Adam of Eynsham, makes much of the tame swan who followed him about his home, as does Giraldus Cambrensis in his slightly later *Vita*, and the faithful swan matured into Hugh's iconographical attribute. Hugh died on November 17, 1200, at the London residence of the bishops of Lincoln (Lincoln's Inn) having charged Geoffrey de Noyers, constructor of Lincoln Cathedral, to complete the chapel of John the Baptist in readiness for his burial. He was canonized by Pope Honorius III in 1220 and translated to a new shrine in the Angel Choir in 1280.

Ignatius of Loyola
1491-1556
Founder of the Society of Jesus
Feast day July 31

Born into a noble Basque family at the castle of Loyola (Guipúzcoa, Spain), Ignatius trained as a soldier and was recruited into the army of the Duke of Nájera, but was seriously wounded at the siege of Pamplona in 1521. Several months of agonizing surgery were only partly successful and he was left with a pronounced limp. He spent his convalescence reading a series of lives of the saints, decided to devote his life to Christian service, and spent a year in solitary penance at Manresa (Catalonia), where he began writing the *Spiritual Exercises*. In 1523 he undertook a pilgrimage to Jerusalem, and on his return embarked on a studentship which took in Barcelona, Alcala, and the universities of Salamanca and Paris.

Ignatius graduated with a master's degree from Paris in 1534, and while there attracted a group of six fellow-students, Francis Xavier among them, all of whom pledged poverty, chastity and service to the Church. They reassembled in Venice three years later with the intention of travelling to the Holy Land but, because of war, were

LEFT: *Ignatius of Loyola* by Peter Paul Rubens.

unable to charter a ship, and were instead ordained priests. Subsequently they offered their services to Pope Paul III in any capacity he saw fit. In 1540 the Pope finally approved the foundation of the Society of Jesus (better known as the Jesuits), with a remit to teach the young, preach among the unconverted, and stand ready to act on the papacy's behalf wherever and whenever required.

For the next 16 years Ignatius directed the growth of the order from Rome. Initially concerned with missionary work, it was from 1547 increasingly invoked by the papacy as an instrument with which to challenge the Protestant reformers of northern Europe. Educational work also began to flourish, each Jesuit rigorously schooled in the methods, and selflessness, of Ignatius' *Spiritual Exercises*. By his death in 1566, there were over one thousand Jesuits working in Europe, India, China, Japan, West Africa, and Brazil.

Isidore of Seville *c.560-636*
Bishop and encyclopedist
Feast day April 4

Isidore was born to a noble family in Seville and educated by his brother, Leander, at a monastery in the city. Leander eventually became Archbishop of Seville, and it seems Isidore succeeded him in about 600. Isidore's concerns as archbishop seem to have been to strengthen the Spanish church by organizing councils and establishing schools and religious houses, convert the sizeable Jewish community of southern Spain to Christianity, and to persuade the few remaining Arians to renounce their faith. In this, and in all his writings, Isidore presents the Church as a unifying force in a fractured country. Scholars are divided on the accuracy of Isidore's portrait of early medieval Spain, but the Visigothic king Reccared's conversion from Arian to Catholic Christianity in 589 certainly presented him

ABOVE: Shrine of St. Isidore of Seville. The rededication of an old nunnery in Léon to San Isidoro in 1063 was the occasion for the solemn translation of the relics of St. Isidore into this reliquary shrine. The shrine, commissioned by Fernando I and Doña Sancha, consists of a wooden core, faced with silver and gilded plaques, and lined with an early medieval silk.

with an opportunity to indulge in a little subtle rhetoric. His most famous historical works are the *Chronica Majora*, a history of the world from the Creation to 615 AD, and the *Historia Regibus Gothorum, Vandalorum et Suevorum*, an invaluable source for the history of the Vandals, Suevi and Visigoths. Isidore's presidency of the church councils of Seville in 619 and Toledo in 633 was also instrumental in the establishment of cathedral schools in Spain.

To a later medieval audience, what impressed was the eclecticism of Isidore's learning. Bede translated part of his *De Natura Rerum*, but the great standard was Isidore's *Etymologiae*. This is a sort of universal medieval encyclopedia, with entries covering medicine, arithmetic, grammar, rhetoric, history, liturgy, theology and natural science. Parts of it were incorporated into the *Bestiary* during the twelfth century, and it remained popular throughout the Middle Ages. It was undoubtedly this popularity that lay behind the arrival of the relics of St. Isidore in León (Castile) in 1063. The story behind this acquisition is a good example of the sort of "visionary discovery" common in medieval hagiographies. According to this, Fernando I of Castile was promised the body of St. Justin by the king of Seville, and sent Alvito, Bishop of León, to fetch it. Unfortunately the body was nowhere to be found, but Isidore obligingly appeared in a vision instead, disclosing his burial place and predicting that Alvito would die in seven days time. The relics were found; Alvito died; and Ordoño, his captain and the Bishop of Astorga, returned with them to León, where they were enshrined in a church rededicated as San Isidoro on December 21, 1063.

James the Great *Died 44* AD
Apostle and martyr Feast day July 25

Brother of John and son of Zebedee. Often called James the Great to distinguish him from another apostle named James (called "the Less"). Luke maintains that James and John fished on the Sea of Tiberias in partnership with Peter, and were among the first of the apostles to be called. Although he is given less prominence in the gospel narratives than either Peter or John, James was nevertheless part of the "inner group" who were privileged to witness the Raising of Jairus' daughter, the Transfiguration, and the Agony in the Garden. He is also recorded as the first apostle to be martyred for his faith,

having been "put to the sword" by Herod Agrippa in Jerusalem, immediately before the arrest of Peter.

The text of the Greek *Acta* purporting to relate the life of James after the Ascension of Christ is almost certainly eighth century, and although there are a few earlier mentions of James, none of these are particularly early. The fourth-century *Breviarum Apostolorum* simply notes that James preached "in Hierusalem" (Jerusalem), while a Greek document maintains that he was buried "at Anchaion in Marmarica" (North Africa). The legend that James evanglized and was buried in Spain depends on a scribal misreading of these texts, "Hieru-

ABOVE: St. James writing an epistle, sixteenth-century German woodcut. James sports the wide-brimmed hat and cockleshell of a pilgrim to his own shrine at Compostela.

RIGHT: *St. James the Great Conquering the Moors*, Giambattista Tiepolo. Tiepolo's mid-eighteenth century portrayal of James shows his miraculous appearance at the early medieval battle of Clavijo.

salem" becoming "Hispaniam" in a seventh-century document and "Anchaion in Marmarica" contracting to "in arca marmorica" (in a marble tomb). The psychological background to the discovery of his tomb was laid by Beatus of Liébana, whose celebrated edition of and commentary on the Apocalypse, *c.*770, compounded these scribal errors and commended St. James as the "Apostle of Spain."

The site of the supposed tomb of St. James was eventually discovered in 813, after a hermit named Pelayo informed Teodomir, Bishop of Iria Flavia (modern Padrón, on the west coast of Galicia) of a vision in which a star had guided him to the tomb, set in the flank of a hill some 20 miles north-east of Iria Flavia. Teodomir opened the tomb to reveal three bodies, believed to be those of James and the two disciples who brought him to Spain. Alfonso II visited the site shortly after 814, and by 838 the feast of St. James was mentioned in the martyrology of Floris de Lyon. Thereafter the growth of a pilgrimage was rapid, with provision for a hospice at Orense mentioned as early as 891, and Godescalc, Bishop of Le Puy, bringing 200 monks to visit the shrine in 951.

Any interpretation of the development of a cult of St. James in Spain is beset by problems, not least the probable displacement of many of the ninth-century legends by a twelfth-century explosion of popular accounts of the exploits of St. James, Charlemagne, and other pilgrims, warriors, or kings. The site of the tomb was referred to as Compostela, and explained to all who would listen as meaning *campus stellae*, or field of the star, but recent excavations have established that the area immediately east of the shrine accommodated a sizeable Roman cemetery, and as the Latin "*compostum*" is often used to describe such cemeteries, the latter etymology seems likely. The first church to be built was dedicated to St. James (*Iago* in Spanish, hence Santiago), raised to the status of cathedral in 1090, and given metropolitan status in 1120, by which time the burgeoning town itself had begun to use the name Santiago de Compostela.

The most popular account of James in Spain was composed in the early twelfth century, and is contained in a composite volume, donated to the cathedral of Santiago de Compostela at some point between 1139 and *c.*1155, and known as the *Liber Sancti Jacobi* (also occasionally called the *Codex Calixtinus*). According to this, James traveled to Spain after the Ascension of Christ, preaching with little success until the Virgin Mary appeared to him at Zaragoza, standing on a pillar and surrounded by a choir of angels. Around this pillar James built a church, which he dedicated to the Virgin. After converting and baptizing many, he then returned to Jerusalem, where he was beheaded by Herod Agrippa

LEFT: *St. James.* Carlo Crivelli's late fifteenth-century image of St. James rests on a conflation of the writer of epistles with the pilgrim.

in 44 AD. His disciples managed to remove his head and body to Jaffa, where they took ship and traveled to Iria Flavia, the voyage being accomplished in one week, certain proof of its miraculous nature. The Roman authorities jailed the party as they landed, but they were released by an angel, whereupon the wife of a local tribal leader, Lupa, ordered the body of James to be buried on a hill terrorized by a celebrated snake. Far from poisoning the disciples, the snake perished on seeing the sign of the cross, and Lupa converted to Christianity. The body of James was then allowed burial in a stone coffin, to be joined some years later by the bodies of his two disciples.

The legend was far from universally accepted, even by those who undertook the pilgrimage. Andrew Boorde, Bishop of Chichester, journeyed to Compostela in the 1520s, and recounted being told by a priest giving absolution in the cathedral at Santiago that there were no relics in the city at all, Charlemagne having removed them all to Toulouse. But this is really secondary to what such journeys signified to the medieval mind, and the pilgrimage to Santiago enjoyed immense popularity throughout the Middle Ages, its status rivalling that of a journey to Jerusalem or Rome.

Jerome *c.342-420*
Doctor of the Church
Feast day September 30

Jerome was born at Strido, near Aquileia (north-east Italy), and educated in Rome. After completing his studies under the grammarian Donatus, Jerome undertook a course in rhetoric, being baptized into the Christian faith some time before 366, while still in Rome. He subsequently traveled in Italy and Gaul, settling to a monastic life with a group of friends in Aquileia, before an acrimonious dispute forced him to leave, and with a number of companions he embarked for Palestine. Illness prevented them from getting any further than Antioch, which they reached in 374. There Jerome experienced a dream in which he was chastized by God for following Cicero, rather than Christ. His response was to spend several years living as a hermit in the Syrian desert, while he devoted himself to learning Hebrew. His return to Antioch was marked by his ordination as a priest, and in about 380 Jerome moved to Constantinople to study under the brilliant theologian Gregory of Nazianzus, where he wrote his

first scriptural treatise, a *Commentary on Isaiah*.

Between 382 and 385 Jerome worked as secretary to Pope Damasus in Rome, an immensely productive time in which, among other projects, he began work on his revisions of the earlier Latin texts of the Bible in order to produce an authoritative and standard version. The revision of the Gospels was completed in 384, but Jerome's relationship with a group of ascetic Christian widows, St. Paula among them, caused a scandal. In 385, amidst a welter of allegations and counter-allegations, he left Rome for Palestine once more. This time Jerome settled in Bethlehem, where he established a monastery for men and encouraged Paula to build a convent for women. The rest of his life was spent here, much of the time devoted to translating the Hebrew Old Testa-

ABOVE: *Jerome in his Cell*, woodcut of 1511 by Albrecht Dürer. This image of Jerome can be compared with that of Ambrose produced in late fifteenth-century Basle (p.15). The lion is crucial as a means of identifying the subject as Jerome; if both were removed, the interior would function as a meditation on scholarship and the passing of time. Dürer's inclusion of an hourglass brings the image even closer to the early *vanitas* paintings then just emerging in the Low Countries.

LEFT: *St. Jerome with SS Christopher and Augustine*, Giovanni Bellini. This altarpiece was given to the church of San Giovanni Crisostomo, Venice, by Giorgio Diletti, a wealthy merchant who lived in the parish and was a member of the Scuola Grande di San Marco. He entrusted its execution to Giovanni Bellini, a fellow-member of the Scuola, and it is as Bellini's last altarpiece, completed in 1513, that the painting is best known. Jerome is seen before a book, one of his translations of the Psaltar perhaps, while an inscription in Greek can be read on the underside of the arch. The text is from Psalm 14: "The Lord looks down from heaven upon the children of men, to see if there are any that act wisely, that seek after God."

ment into Latin. Previous Latin versions of the Old Testament had been translated from the Greek *Septuagint*, itself a translation. Indeed, Jerome's own *Gallican Psalter* of *c*.392 was taken from the Greek. But the great Hebrew translation was added to Jerome's earlier revision of the Gospels and some earlier texts of the *Epistles* and *Revelation*, becoming known as the *Vulgate*. It was the standard Latin Bible of the Middle Ages and beyond.

Jerome's later life was occupied by a dazzling correspondence with the likes of Rufinus of Aquileia and **Augustine of Hippo**, and with writing a series of polemics against heresy. He died in 420, to be buried in the church of the Nativity at Bethlehem, his body laid close to the tomb of Paula. Later representations of Jerome usually show him wearing a cardinal's hat and with a lion at his feet, both of them medieval interpolations. The cardinal's hat first turns up in the thirteenth century, on the spurious assumption that Pope Damasus created him a "Prince of the Church." The lion is a more intriguing tale, but so resembles the classical story of Androcles and the lion that it is almost certainly a medieval annexation. Nonetheless the story has a charm which bears repetition, and is related by Jacopo da Voragine in the *Golden Legend*. Here we are told that while Jerome sat with the brethren in the monastery at Bethlehem, a lion appeared, limping horribly. The monks fled, but Jerome noticed the lion had a thorn embedded in a paw and calmly re-moved the thorn. The grateful lion adopted Jerome as a companion, but Jerome was convinced that all members of the monastery should have a role, and gave the lion the task of guarding the ass who fetched wood daily for the monks. All went well until the day when the lion fell asleep, and the unguarded ass was seized by bandits. When he awoke to find the ass missing, the lion returned to the monastery, where the monks surveyed his doleful countenance and assumed that he had devoured the ass. Their punishment was to refuse him his daily portion of food, and to order him to do the work of the ass in atonement. This he did in perfect humility, until one day he noticed the ass marching along in a passing caravan, captured bandits and ass alike, and triumphantly returned to the monastery to prove his innocence.

Joan of Arc *1412-31*
The Maid of Orléans or Jeanne la Pucelle, literally Joan the Maid
Feast day May 30

Born and raised to a poor farming family in Domrémy (Champagne), Joan experienced the first of her famous transcendental visitations in 1425, describing it as a voice accompanied by searing light. Over time these "voices" increased in number, among which Joan claimed to distinguish SS Michael, Catherine of Alexandria and Margaret of Antioch, who persuaded her of her mission to save France.

LEFT: Logis Royal, Loches (Indre-et-Loire, France). The Logis Royal witnessed the meeting of Joan of Arc and the future Charles VII in June, 1429. Joan's famous petition, "Noble Dauphin, do not listen to these counsels, so numerous and so long. Rather you should come quickly to Rheims, to claim the crown which is your right," was delivered in the late fourteenth-century great hall of the Vieux Logis, which is seen here from the north-east.

An attempt in 1428 to convince the French commander at Vaucouleurs of the authenticity and usefulness of her voices failed, but Joan won considerable local support, and in February 1429, in the company of six soldiers, set out from Domrémy to seek an audience with the heir to the French throne, the Dauphin, at Chinon. She arrived on March 6 and lodged in town while waiting for an audience at the château. When one was granted two days later the Dauphin, the future Charles VII, attempted to disguise himself by swapping robes with a courtier. Undeceived by this ruse, Joan addressed Charles directly, saying "The King of Heaven sends words by me that you shall be annointed and crowned in the city of Reims. You are the heir to France and true son of the king." Given that his father was mad and his mother had taken a number of lovers, Charles was notoriously plagued by doubts as to his own legitimacy, but he seems to have been wholly convinced by Joan and, after her case had been examined by a theological court at Poitiers, gave her command of an army. On April 26 she raised her standard at Blois; on May 8 she relieved Orléans; and, having inflicted two serious defeats on the English in June, finally persuaded Charles to accompany her to Reims, where his coronation was celebrated on July 17.

This should have completed her mission, indeed her voices cautioned she did not have long to live, but it seems likely that she became intoxicated by her military successes. A failed autumn attack on Paris was followed by a stand-off, but Joan resumed campaigning in the spring of 1430. It was to prove her undoing. Having relieved Compiègne of occupation by the Burgundian allies of the English, she was captured on May 24 when leading a small party of troops out from one of the city gates. The question of what to do with her remained unresolved for some time, but finally, on November 21, through the mediation of Pierre Cauchon, Bishop of Beauvais, Joan was ransomed for 10,000 ducats and handed over to the English captain of Rouen, Richard of Warwick. She was imprisoned in a tower of Philip Augustus's old castle to the north of the cathedral in Rouen, while Warwick reinforced the city against the possibility of popular uprising. On February 21, 1431, Bishop Cauchon opened the first session of her trial on charges of witchcraft and heresy. The trial lasted three months, and after further examination in her cell, a summary of her statements was compiled. Her visions were pronounced "false and diabolical," and she was found "heretical and schismatic" and led to the scaffold in the cemetery of St-Ouen. The precise nature of events here is a matter of controversy. Encouraged by a large crowd to recant, Joan did make some sort of repudiation of her former testimony. What form this took is uncertain, but it was enough to convince the English to commute her sentence to one of life imprisonment. Cauchon's determination was not to be brooked, however, and on Trinity Sunday her English captors tricked her into wearing a man's clothes in the prison courtyard, thus breaking a vow it was said she made on recanting her crimes. On May 30 she was led to the Place du Vieux-Marché and burned at the stake as a witch, the terrified English guards throwing her unconsumed heart into the river Seine. The zeal with which her captors pursued her death is a measure of the influence she exercised, and the whispered misgivings of the English soldiery eroded their already tenuous belief in an English future in northern France. In 1449 Charles VII entered Rouen unopposed and, with the help of the Franciscan Hélie de Bourdeilles, set in motion the procedures which led to Pope Callixtus III declaring Joan innocent in 1456. She was formally canonized by Pope Benedict XV in 1920, and recognized as the second patron of France, after the great medieval protector of France, St. Denis.

Joan is usually depicted fully armed and the sources attest to her wearing a suit of white armor. The 1431 trial deposition records that she refused the sword Charles offered her at Chinon, and instead despatched soldiers to fetch her a sword from the pilgrimage chapel of Ste-Catherine-de-Fierbois (Indre-et-Loire): "The best is found behind the altar of Ste-Catherine which I much love. You will find it easily, it is marked with five crosses." The chapel of Ste-Catherine was believed to have been founded by Charles Martel, the grandfather of Charlemagne; it was thought he left his sword there in thanksgiving after his great victory over the Moors in 732. By about 1380 a tradition had grown up that knights returning from battle would also offer a sword to the chapel. It was almost certainly one of these, a late-fourteenth-century sword, that Joan wielded, but from this grew the legend that Joan fought with the sword of Charles Martel, a powerful connection to make in late medieval France.

FAR LEFT: Gilded statue of Joan of Arc (Paris, nineteenth-century). Joan is seen fully armed, and carrying the standard she first raised at Blois on April 26, 1429.

John the Apostle
First century
Apostle Feast day December 27

John is traditionally thought to be the author of the Fourth Gospel, the *Book of Revelation* and three New Testament *Epistles*. The so-called synoptic gospels (those bearing the names of Matthew, Mark and Luke) identify John as one of the sons of Zebedee and the brother of James, who worked as a fisherman on the Sea of Tiberias before being called to become an apostle of Christ. He belonged to that small "inner group" of disciples who witnessed the Raising of Jairus' Daughter, the Transfiguration of Christ, and the Agony in the Garden. Like his brother James, he was evidently passionate and quick-tempered, and on a number of occasions Christ refers to them both as "Boanerges" (sons of thunder). After the Ascension, John developed a close relationship with Peter, and *Acts of the Apostles* frequently mentions the two together. They shared imprisonment in Jerusalem, conducting a joint defence before the Sanhedrin, and were asked by the other apostles to work together in bringing the Holy Spirit to the new converts of Samaria.

The fourth gospel never mentions John by name, nor indeed does it identify its author, but the Prologue can be interpreted as meaning the writer was a witness to the events he describes. The identification of this author as John is extremely early, and the view is shared by such noted late second-century writers as Clement of Alexandria and Irenaeus, and the discovery of an early fragment of chapter 18, the *Rylands St. John Papyrus* (John Rylands Library, Manchester), suggests the gospel was written before 120 AD. The view that it was written by John the Apostle rests on the assumption that the witness referred to as "the disciple whom Jesus loved" was John. This disciple certainly appears where one might expect to find John but, as so many of the events narrated in the synoptic gospels are absent, the evidence is far from conclusive. Nevertheless, "the disciple whom Jesus loved" was present at the Last Supper, where he lay on the breast of Christ; stood at the foot of the Cross and was entrusted with the care of the Virgin Mary; and was the first to recognize the Resurrected Christ at the Sea of Tiberias.

The sophisticated exegesis, spirituality,

and discursive style of the fourth gospel is quite different from the narrative concerns of the three other gospels (Matthew, Mark and Luke), and a number of theologians have argued that it presupposes, on the part of the reader, a knowledge of the principal events of the life of Christ as related in the synoptic gospels. It is largely because of its wrestling with philosophical questions of Faith, Resurrection, and Eternal Life, that its impact on later Christian thought was so profound. And although modern scholarship is inclined to see it as having been written by a disciple of John, rather than John himself, relatively few dismiss the case for the fourth gospel as a direct reflection of his teaching. That teaching is likely to have been conducted in Ephesus, for the tradition that John settled at Ephesus in Asia Minor (modern Turkey), was exiled to the island of Patmos by the Emperor Domitian in the early 90 AD, and returned to Ephesus, where he died *c*.100 AD, is again very early.

ABOVE: St John seen as author of the Fourth Gospel; prefatory Evangelist portrait from a Carolingian gospel book.

RIGHT ABOVE: *The Assumption of John the Evangelist* (Giotto: Peruzzi chapel, Sta Croce, Florence). Giotto's rendering of an unusual scene probably dates from *c*.1325.

RIGHT BELOW: Deposition group, San Joan de les Abadesses. This striking group of painted wooden figures was installed in the Catalan church of San Joan in 1251. John stands between the bad thief and Nicodemus.

John the Baptist
Died c.30 AD
Forerunner of Jesus Christ Feast days
June 24 (nativity) and August 29
(decollation)

John was the son of Zacharias, a priest at the Temple of Jerusalem, and Elizabeth, a cousin of the Virgin Mary. The couple were childless and Elizabeth was past child-bearing age. The story of John's birth is recounted by Luke, who speaks of the visit of the angel Gabriel to Zacharias: "Fear not, Zacharias; for thy prayer is heard; and thy wife Elizabeth shall bear thee a son, and thou shalt call his name John."

It seems likely that John was in his mid-20s when he began preaching in Judaea, a ministry which is reported in similar terms in all four gospels. Mark describes it as "The voice of one crying in the wilderness, Prepare ye the way of the Lord, make his paths straight. John did baptize in the wilderness, and preach the baptism of re-

pentance for the remission of sins." John's way of life was based on that of the more ascetic Old Testament prophets, clothed in "camel's hair" and eating locusts and wild honey, but his teaching was of the imminence of the Messiah: "I indeed baptize you with water; but one mightier than I cometh, the latchet of whose shoes I am unworthy to unloose: He shall baptize you with the Holy Ghost."

An immensely charismatic figure, John attracted a number of followers, the future apostle Andrew among them, all of whom he baptized in the river Jordan. According to John's gospel, it was while he was at Bethabara that John met Jesus. He greeted him with the words, "Behold the Lamb of God, which taketh away the sin of the world," and then baptized him. Shortly afterward he was imprisoned, for denouncing the incestuous union between Herod Antipas and Herodias, and although he was able to communicate with Christ from prison, as recorded by Luke, Matthew reports his death before the narrative of the Feeding of

BELOW: *The Beheading of John the Baptist* by Pierre Puvis de Chavannes, the foremost French mural painter of the later nineteenth century.

RIGHT: *The Baptism of Christ*, Piero della Francesca. Piero situates the Baptism in a valley close to his home town of Borgo San Sepolcro, on the borders of Tuscany and Umbria. The man pulling off his shirt in the background, his head covered, serves as a reminder that baptism is a casting off of the old Adam and an embracing the new. The painting is undated, but perhaps belongs to the 1450s.

the Five Thousand. The gospels lay the blame for his execution squarely on Herodias. After Salome, the daughter of Herodias, had pleased Herod with her dancing at his birthday feast, Herod promised her whatever she wished "unto the half of my kingdom." "And she went forth, and said unto her mother, What shall I ask? And [Herodias] said, The head of John the Baptist" (Mark 6$^{23\text{-}24}$). Not without regret, Herod sent an executioner to deal with John in prison, and the severed head was brought to Salome on a platter. Thus, as Augustine writes, an oath rashly made was criminally kept.

The *Antiquities* of Josephus identifies the place of John's death as the fort of Machaerus on the Dead Sea, but an early tradition asserts he was buried at Sebaste (Samaria), where his tomb was despoiled by Emperor Julian the Apostate in about 362. Thereafter his relics seem to have been dispersed, and during the Middle Ages the best part of a dozen churches claimed possession of his head. His cult is both early and significant, however, and two of the Fathers of the Church, **Augustine of Hippo** and **Jerome**,

lay great stress on the celebration of the feast of his nativity. John's role as the herald of Christ and his institution of the sacrament of baptism were of fundamental importance for the development of the Church.

FAR LEFT: John the Baptist preaching in the wilderness, a nineteenth-century view.

ABOVE LEFT: The Baptism of Christ engraved on a Carolingian rock crystal. Engraved rock crystals were an extremely popular, if expensive, vehicle for narrative imagery at the Carolingian court. The Rouen crystal is unusual in featuring the Baptism of Christ, and was probably engraved in Metz *c*.860. The inclusion of an angel holding a cloth derived from early Christian sources.

LEFT : The Baptism of Christ, Arian Baptistry, Ravenna. This mosaic is at the center of the dome of the Arian bapristry (now known as Sta Maria in Cosmedin), and was probably designed in the reign of Theodoric the Ostrogoth *c*.495 AD. Christ is represented as a decidedly boyish figure, while John the Baptist wears a cloak of camel's hair, and the personification of the river Jordan is bizarrely embellished with a pair of lobster-claws on his head.

John Chrysostom
347-407
Patriarch Feast day September 13 (West), November 13 (East)

Born to an army family in Antioch, John was educated in law by the noted pagan orator Libanius, and in Christian theology by Diodore of Tarsus. Between *c.*373 and 381 he lived as a hermit in the mountains above Antioch, but returned to the city as his health began to fail, where he served as a deacon. After his ordination as priest in 386, Bishop Flavian took him on as an assistant, giving him the responsibility of instructing the poor in the Scriptures. His sermons earned him the epithet *chrysostom* (golden-mouthed), and during the late 380s and 390s he wrote the *Homilies* on *Genesis, John* and, above all, the *Epistles*, for which he is best remembered. The importance of the *Homilies* lies with their clear exposition of spiritual truth and practical meaning, and like other theologians of the "Antioch School," John denied the validity of the allegorical interpretation of Scripture.

His reputation as a strong opponent of imperial corruption led Emperor Arcadius to obtain John's election as Patriarch of Constantinople in 398, an appointment which caused his death. His attempts at a moral reform of both the clergy and the court invited the hostility of Empress Eudoxia, while Theophilus, Patriarch of Alexandria, exploited the situation to avenge his disappointment at not having gained the see of Constantinople himself. In July, 403, at Chalcedon, Theophilus packed a synod with aggrieved Syrian and Egyptian bishops, and had John condemned on 29 counts, including the charge of treason for having described Eudoxia as "Jezebel." The accusations were trumped-up, but John was briefly sent into exile, before an earthquake seems to have worried the court into recalling him to Constantinople. John's resumption of the attack on lax morality, prostitution and favoritism at court, and on Jewish traders in the city, prompted Eudoxia and Theophilus to have him thrown out once more on a trumped-up charge. His banishment to Cucusus in Armenia was opposed by the Western Church, but the petitions proved fruitless and John eventually died on the road to the southern Black Sea coast, exhausted by a deliberate regime of forced bad-weather marches on foot.

John of the Cross *1542-91*
Carmelite friar and mystic
Feast day December 14

Born Juan de Yepes, he joined the Carmelites at Medina del Campo (Castile) in 1563, before being sent to study theology at Salamanca, where he was ordained a priest in 1567. Dissuaded by Theresa of Ávila from joining the Carthusian order, John adopted Theresa's Carmelite reform and attached himself to the first of the new *discalced* (barefoot) houses for men at Duruelo. In 1572 he became confessor to the Carmelite nuns at Ávila, but was arrested following the

ABOVE: St. John of the Cross, Carmelite convent of San Juan de la Cruz, Sanlúcar la Mayor, Andalucia. Detail of an eighteenth-century retable showing John of the Cross inspired by the Holy Spirit.

1575 Carmelite General Chapter at Piacenza and imprisoned in Toledo, the Chapter having refused to recognize the Discalced reform. He escaped from prison within a year and made his way south, founding a college at Baeza (Andalusia) in 1579, and subsequently acting as prior at Granada and Segovia. The Discalced Carmelites were in fact recognized in 1580, but John came to disagree with the policies of Nicolás Doria, Reformist Vicar General, and toward the end of his life was banished to Úbeda (Andalusia), where he died in 1591.

These few spare details of John's movements formed the background to the writing of some of the most moving religious and mystical poetry ever to emerge from Europe, much of it written in conditions of appalling hardship. A small man, who seems to have captivated most who met him with his generosity and warm-heartedness, John fell foul of the ecclesiastical politics of sixteenth-century Spain. Yet the poems he began writing while in prison in Toledo, *The Spiritual Canticle, Ascent of Mount Carmel* (or *Dark Night of the Soul*) and *Living Flame of Love,* have a quite extraordinary ease and beauty. All have been translated into English, most recently by Roy Campbell.

Joseph *First century*
Husband of Virgin Mary
Feast days March 19 and May 1

The carpenter from Nazareth, Joseph was betrothed to the **Virgin Mary** at the time of the Annunciation. Joseph's understandable misgivings at finding his fiancée with child were allayed by the appearance of an angel in a dream, and the marriage was celebrated before the Roman census took the couple from Nazareth to Bethlehem, where Mary gave birth to Jesus. Subsequent angelic interventions were also responsible for Joseph's decision to take the family into Egypt, to avoid King Herod's massacre of new-born children, and their return to Nazareth after the death of Herod. The role he plays in searching for the 12-year-old Jesus after the feast of the Passover (*Luke* 2^{42-52}) is the last significant mention of Joseph in the New Testament, and completes the gospel portrait of him as a just, loyal and practical foster-father and husband.

The mid-second-century *Protoevangelium of James* maintains that Joseph was already an old man at the time of the birth of Christ, perhaps because John implies he was dead by the time of the Crucifixion (he speaks of the Virgin Mary being taken into the home of "the disciple whom Jesus loved"), but on the whole this seems unlikely. The medieval cult of Joseph was only widespread in the East, where the fifth- to seventh-century *History of Joseph the Carpenter* enjoyed a large audience. In the West interest was localized, and in the majority of surviving medieval mystery plays Joseph is essentially a figure of fun. The great Counter-Reformation divines, **Ignatius of Loyola** and **Theresa of Ávila**, were principally responsible for the renewal of his cult in southern Europe and its diffusion to the New World. By this date, the emphasis had begun to change, and the promise of comfort to all who act in the name of Joseph, a promise contained in the *History of Joseph the Carpenter*, led to his adoption by innumerable convents and hospitals.

BELOW: *The Holy Family in the Carpenter's Workshop*. Rembrandt's ink and wash drawing of the 1630s shows Joseph bent over his workbench; as in most representations he is depicted at some distance from the Virgin and Child.

RIGHT: *The Presentation in the Temple and the Flight into Egypt*. Joseph is seen as a swarthy Flemish peasant in Melchior Broederlam's stunning painting of 1393-94.

Joseph of Arimathea
First century
Jewish counsellor Feast day March 17

And behold, there was a man named Joseph, a counsellor; and he was a good man, and just: (The same had not consented to the counsel and deed of them;) he was of Arimathea, a city of the Jews; who also himself waited for the kingdom of God. This man went unto Pilate, and begged the body of Jesus. And he took it down, and wrapped it in linen, and laid it in a sepulchre that was hewn in stone, wherein never man before was laid. (*Luke* 23[50-53]).

All four canonical gospels agree that Joseph of Arimathea took Christ down from the cross and laid him in the tomb, John adding that he was "a disciple of Jesus, but secretly for fear of the Jews."

The later accounts are legion. Joseph is given prominence in the fourth-century *Acts of Pilate*, where he is credited with founding the first church at Lydda. The most popular story, in south-west England at least, associates Joseph with the foundation of Glastonbury and the bringing of the Holy Grail to Britain. This first appears in a version of William of Malmesbury's *De Antiquitate Glastoniensis Ecclesiae* (*On the Antiquity of Glastonbury Churches*), probably written about 25 years after the 1191 "discovery" of the body of King Arthur. Here we are told that Joseph was sent from Gaul by Philip the Apostle to bring Christianity to the British, and to ease this task he

carried the Grail. He was received with honor and given the island of Yniswitrin (Glastonbury), where he built a church of wattle which he dedicated to the Virgin Mary.

The Grail Legend is inextricably entangled with Glastonbury's claim to Arthur, although, intriguingly, John of Glastonbury's *Legenda* of c.1400 makes no mention of the Grail. Late medieval representations of Joseph's gifts to Glastonbury show, not so much the Grail, as two silver vessels which housed the blood and sweat of Christ. This may well be connected with the seventh-century account of a phial of the precious blood of Christ, which had been washed ashore after Isaac of Arimathea, Joseph's nephew, had entrusted it "to the sea and the mercy of God," and was preserved in the abbey of La Trinité, Fécamp (Normandy).

Lawrence *Died 258*
Martyr Feast day August 10

One of the seven deacons of Rome under Pope Sixtus II, Lawrence was martyred, some four days after Sixtus, during the persecution of Emperor Valerian. The tradition that he was roasted on a gridiron is early, but is regarded as untenable by classical scholars and was probably lifted from the account of the martyrdom of Vincent of Saragossa, who died under Diocletian in 304. Ambrose records the story that when Lawrence was asked to surrender the treasure of the Church, he rounded up some of the poor of Rome and presented them to the Roman authorities with the words: "These are the treasure of the Church."

There is no doubt, however, that after his martyrdom Lawrence was buried in a catacomb along the Via Tiburtina, where a sizeable tomb chamber was excavated around the grave to act as a *martyrium*. A cylindrical shaft was then sunk above the tomb, to allow the Christian faithful to place offerings on the grave, or to lower strips of cloth which might acquire a reliquary power through touching the martyr, somewhat in the manner of the early tomb of St. Peter on the Vatican hill. Constantine added a large funerary basilica to the south of the tomb in about 330, while between 579 and 590 Pope Pelagius II authorized the leveling of the hill in which the catacomb had been tunneled, to allow a galleried basilica to be constructed over the shrine itself. This is the surviving church of San Lorenzo fuori le Mura.

Lazarus *First century*
Brother of Mary and Martha Feast day December 17

Lazarus was the brother of Mary and **Martha** of Bethany, and was raised from the dead by Jesus. Although Luke mentions the house of Mary and Martha, he makes no mention of Lazarus and the New Testament account of him is confined to John. A fairly late account of his life, originating in the eastern Mediterranean, maintains that after the Crucifixion of Christ, Lazarus was taken to Jaffa by hostile Jews and cast adrift in a leaky boat, in the hope that he would drown. Miraculously, he landed in Cyprus and was made Bishop of Kition, where he was buried some 30 years later. Emperor Leo VI claimed to have discovered his relics in 890, and had them translated to Constantinople.

The Western tradition is later still, and has a number of points in common with that then current in the East. According to this, Lazarus was placed in a rudderless boat along with **Mary Magdalen** and Martha, and washed up on the coast of Provence. Here he was made Bishop of Marseille, preaching and baptizing many, before he fell foul of Domitian's persecution and was martyred in about 95 AD. The Provençal accounts maintain that he was buried in a shallow cave near Aix-en-Provence, over which the church of St-Victoire was subsequently built, though this belief is likely to have been prompted by the burial of another Lazarus, a fifth-century bishop of Aix, in the same church.

The main Western pilgrimage center was St-Lazare at Autun, although how Lazarus came to be venerated in Burgundy is uncertain. The cult predates that of Mary Magdalen at Vézelay, believed in the West to be the sister of Lazarus, but became entwined with it during a bitter late-eleventh-century dispute between Cluny and Autun over rights of visitation at Avallon and Vézelay. In the late 1080s the dedication of the church of Notre-Dame at Avallon was expanded to include St-Lazare, and a gold reliquary containing what was claimed to be the head of Lazarus duly appeared in the church. In 1100 Norgaud, Bishop of Autun, forbade all offerings at the shrine of the Magdalen at Vézelay, and in 1103 the monks of Vézelay retaliated by claiming possession of Lazarus in addition to Mary Magdalen. In 1106 Abbot Artaud of Vézelay was assassinated. The quarrel finally came to an end in 1116, when the rights of the bishop and canons of Autun

FAR LEFT ABOVE: *St. Lawrence* (detail), studio of the fifteenth-century Flemish artist Rogier van der Weyden.

FAR LEFT BELOW: *The Martyrdom of St. Lawrence*, by Neri di Biccit. Perspectively uncomfortable fifteenth-century painting which situates Lawrence's gridiron along an arcaded Roman street.

to the church of Avallon were recognized by Cluny, and it was then publicly asserted that the whole of the body of Lazarus was contained in the cathedral of Autun. It is likely to be shortly after this *rapprochement* that Bishop Etienne de Bagé began work on a new pilgrimage church to the south of the cathedral, which was dedicated to St-Lazare on December 28, 1130.

Because he was often confused with the Lazarus of the parable of Dives and Lazarus, whose sores were licked by dogs, Lazarus became the patron of those suffering from diseases of the skin, and the pilgrimages to his shrine at Autun were chiefly undertaken by lepers.

Louis *1214-70*
King of France Feast day August 25

Son of Louis VIII of France and Blanche of Castile, Louis ascended to the French throne on the death of his father in 1226, but remained subject to his mother as regent throughout his minority. In 1234 he married Margaret of Provence, sister of Eleanor, the wife of Henry III of England, and the following year took up the reins of government as Louis IX. His late-thirteenth-century biographer Jean de Joinville, in his *Histoire de St. Louis* saw him as a "just ruler, holy man and chivalrous knight," and he was undoubtedly regarded as a model king by later medieval writers. Even Matthew Paris, notoriously given to English precedent in matters of government, described Louis during the 1250s as "king of earthly kings, both because of his heavenly annointment and because of his power and military prominence."

The reign of Louis IX straddled a period when the pre-eminence of French culture was acknowledged throughout Europe. Its language was the language of the aristocracy, its universities were the intellectual power-houses of the West, and its king was

BELOW: *The Raising of Lazarus* (Giotto: Padua, Arena Chapel). Giotto's electrifying portrayal, part of a larger cycle he painted for Enrico Scrovegni between 1301 and 1306, explicitly compares the raising of Lazarus with God's creation of Adam, which is seen in the quatrefoil to the left.

RIGHT: Sainte Chapelle, Paris (interior to the east). Louis IX's exquisite reliquary chapel, built between 1239 and 1248 to house the Crown of Thorns.

the leader of Christendom. Louis' own contribution to this prestige was considerable, and revolved initially around his perceived piety and justice. In 1239 Louis managed to obtain from his cousin, Baudouin II, Latin Emperor of Constantinople, the relic of Christ's Crown of Thorns, which he received at Villeneuve-l'Archevêque (near Sens, Burgundy). Along with other relics of Christ's Passion, this was enshrined in the Sainte Chapelle, Louis' palace chapel on the Ile-de-la-Cité (Paris). At the consecration of the Sainte Chapelle on April 26, 1248, Pope Innocent IV called Louis "*Rex Christianissimus*" (most Christian King) and averred "Christ has crowned Louis with his crown." This moment must rank among the high points of a Christian concept of kingship.

Sadly, from here the reverses were painful. Later in 1248, Louis took ship to Cyprus to embark on a Crusade. Damietta was taken in 1249, but the battle of Marsuna in 1250 resulted in the rout of the Christian army, and Louis was forced to surrender Damietta, abandon most of the Frankish soldiers, who had fallen prey to disease, and spend the next two years visiting the few holy sites still accessible in Palestine. He returned to France in 1254, chastened by the experience. The later 1250s were marked by a number of considerable achievements: the imposition of peace with Flanders in 1256; the foundation of the Sorbonne in 1257; and the signing of the Treaty of Paris with England in 1259. Jean de Joinville waxes lyrical about these years, drawing attention to Louis' religious works:

Just like the writer who has finished his book and who illuminates it with gold and azure, so the king illuminated his kingdom with the beautiful abbeys he made, and with the great number of hospitals and convents of Dominicans, Franciscans and other religious orders.

Despite the heavy defeat of the earlier Crusade, in 1267 Louis began planning a second attempt at wresting control of the Holy Land from the Saracens. The Crusade did not get under way until July 1, 1270, landing at Tunis, but typhoid struck almost immediately, and on August 25 Louis died. His body was shipped back to Aigues-Mortes, from where a funeral cortege brought it to Paris for solemn burial at St-Denis. The mourning was very real, for in Louis' death France had lost an extraordinarily selfless, determined and equable monarch. He was formally canonized by Pope Boniface VIII in 1297, after which his

grandson, Philip the Fair, raised Louis' body from its tomb at St-Denis, and commissioned a head-shrine for the Sainte Chapelle and a heart-shrine for the new church of St-Louis at Poissy.

Louis of Toulouse *1274-97*
Franciscan preacher and bishop
Feast day August 19

Son of Charles II, Angevin King of Naples and Mary of Hungary, Louis was born at Brignolles (Provence), and after being taken prisoner by Pedro III, King of Aragon, in 1284, spent a number of years in Barcelona. While here he came under the influence of Franciscan teachers. On his release in 1295 Louis refused Jaime II's offer of his Aragonese sister in marriage, renounced all claims to the Neapolitan throne in favor of his brother, Robert, and entered the Franciscan order in Rome. Pope Boniface VIII then consecrated him Bishop of Toulouse early in 1297.

During his short tenure as bishop, Louis continued to live as a Franciscan, preaching

BELOW: Louis of Toulouse, seen in an eighteenth-century engraving.

RIGHT: *The St. Louis Altarpiece* (Simone Martini: Naples, Palazzo Reale di Capodimonte). The altarpiece, commissioned in 1317 to celebrate the canonization of Louis of Toulouse, is a sumptuous dynastic icon. He is seen sacrificing his earthly crown to his brother, Robert of Naples, and thus conferring legitimacy on a dubious Angevin monarchy. But by this date Louis had also become patron of the Franciscan Strict Observants, and his episcopal cloak opens to reveal a simple Franciscan habit.

daily in a threadbare habit and refusing to eat, or offer Mass, from anything other than the simplest vessels. His discomfort with the appointment led him to offer his resignation, and he returned to Brignolles, but died suddenly and was buried by the Franciscans in Marseilles. He was canonized in 1317, the occasion for his brother, Robert of Naples, to commission an altarpiece depicting him from Simone Martini. By this time the cult of Louis of Toulouse had become overtly political, an instrument of Angevin policy in southern Italy, and an ideal of wordly renunciation for the Strict Observants in the battles for the future of the Franciscan order (see **Francis**).

Lucy *Died 304?*
Virgin and martyr
Feast day December 13

Lucy's legend has parallels with that of **Agatha**, and the medieval accounts explicitly link the two, the *Golden Legend* asserting that Agatha appeared in a vision to Lucy and inspired her to take a vow of virginity. Lucy's cult is well represented at an early date, for she is included in the Canons of the Roman Mass and an inscription usually dated to *c.*400 in Syracuse mentions her name. Although not conclusive, these do suggest that the traditional ascription of her martyrdom to Diocletian's persecution

LEFT: *St. Lucy*, fifteenth-century central Italian panel painting. Lucy is here compared to the Virgin Mary, with two angels holding a "cloth of honor" to her rear while a choir of musical angels are seen in the foreground. She holds in her right hand the sword by which she was killed, with the eyes which are her usual attribute implied in the pot she holds to her left.

of 304 is well founded, though once again, as with Agatha, the sixth-century account of her life is almost certainly pure fiction. This casts her as a wealthy citizen of Syracuse, who refused all offers of marriage and was denounced as a Christian to the Roman authorities. The trial judge first ordered that she should be raped in a brothel, but by miraculous intercession her body was locked; then that she should be burned, but the flames could not harm her; and finally that she should be killed by a sword to the throat, which was successful. Later accounts also allege that her eyes were torn out, hence the frequent medieval representations of her holding a dish in which two eyes can be seen. Her name translates as light, however, and she was invoked against failing eyesight before the legend of the loss of her own eyes began to circulate, which sounds like straightforward medieval embroidery.

Luke *First century*
Evangelist Feast day October 18

Paul refers to Luke as a physician, and an early tradition maintains that he was born in Antioch, both assertions consistent with what can be adduced about him elsewhere in the New Testament. Luke wrote both the third gospel and *Acts of the Apostles*, the latter intended as a continuation of the former, and both addressed to "Theophilus" (lover of God). If the sections of *Acts* written in the first person plural are taken to include Luke, he accompanied Paul for part of the Second and Third Missionary Journeys, in Macedonia, the Aegean and Asia Minor. Luke is also mentioned with Mark in Rome during Paul's captivity *c.*60 AD.

Luke opens his gospel with a statement of intent, drawing attention to his reliance on "eyewitnesses" and asserting that, once finished, the reader might "know the certainty of those things, wherein thou hast been instructed." It is certainly the most eloquent of the synoptic gospels, and in many ways the most moving, for not only is much of the Annunciation story specific to Luke, but the parables of the Good Samaritan, Prodigal Son, and Dives and Lazarus also appear nowhere else. The attention Luke devotes to women is equally notable, and the stories of Mary and Martha, Elisabeth, the words of Christ to the women in Jerusalem, the widow of Nain, are all given great prominence. Indeed, if one were to discount those parts of Luke's gospel common to Matthew or Mark, the emphasis is very much on women, the poor, Gentiles, the difficulties faced by the Roman authorities, and the universal compassion of Christ.

A late-second-century document is responsible for the belief that Luke wrote his gospel in Greece, where he died, unmarried, at the age of 84. His supposed relics were identified at Thebes (Boeotia) by Emperor Constantius II, *c.*356, while Constantius was collecting apostolic relics for the Church of the Holy Apostles, Constantinople, though possession was disputed between Padua and Constantinople during the later Middle Ages. Luke's symbol, the calf or ox, was justified by Jerome in his *Prologue to the Gospels* in an attempt to prove the validity of only four "canonical" gospels. According to this argument the vision of the *Tetramorph*, the four beasts described in the *Book of Revelation* as "like" a lion, calf, man and eagle, signified the four Evangelists, and as Luke opens his gospel with the Sacrifice in the Temple, and the beast of sacrifice is a calf or ox, the symbol was his.

BELOW: *St. Luke with a Portrait of the Virgin and Child*, by El Greco. The belief that Luke painted, or carved, a portrait of the Virgin and Child gained currency during the twelfth century, and is responsible for the dedication of painters' guilds to St. Luke. El Greco's late sixteenth-century portrayal is among the last examples of what, in the fifteenth century, was a fashionable subject.

Magi *First century*
Wise men Feast day July 23

The three Magi were described by Matthew as wise men from the East, who brought gifts of gold, frankincense, and myrrh to the new-born "King of the Jews." As they were the first Gentiles to adore Christ, they assumed considerable importance among early theologians, and the feast of *Epiphany* (meaning "manifestation") on January 6 was associated in the Latin West with the Adoration of the Magi from the fourth century, and not, as in the East, with Christ's Baptism. The early-third-century writer Tertullian is thought to be the first to describe the Magi as "Kings," while a sixth-century Roman text, subsequently followed by Bede, gives them the names Caspar, Melchior and Balthasar.

By the seventh century the Magi were accounted saints, though attempts to establish the origins of the reliquary cult have not proved successful. Their relics were certainly in Milan by the early Middle Ages, where it was said they were obtained from fifth-century Constantinople. Frederick Barbarossa's conquest of Milan in 1164 led to the presentation of the relics to Reinald von Dassel, Archbishop of Cologne, who took them north for enshrinement in Cologne Cathedral. The Magi were subsequently placed in a magnificent new reliquary, the Three Kings Shrine, designed by Nicholas of Verdun some time after 1181 which, though damaged, survives in the present cathedral.

Magnus of Orkney
Died 1116
Martyr Feast day April 16

Son of Erlend Thorfinnson, one of two Norse chieftains who ruled the Orkneys. Magnus (Erlendson) was taken prisoner by Magnus Barefoot, King of Norway, after his conversion to Christianity, and forced to join the Norse raiding parties then harrying the coast of north-western England. He managed to escape and was given sanctuary at the court of King Malcolm III of Scotland *c.*1090, but following Malcolm's death in 1093 he determined to devote himself to a life of penitential prayer. Magnus only returned to the Orkneys after the death of Magnus Barefoot, ostensibly to rule jointly with his cousin Haakon, but he became the

BELOW: The Magi follow the star to Bethlehem, detail from a psalter of *c.*1140.

RIGHT ABOVE: St. Magnus, Egilsay (Orkney). Although the relics of St. Magnus were translated to Kirkwall Cathedral, a church was built on Egilsay, where he was killed, during the twelfth century.

RIGHT BELOW: The Three Magi (Ravenna, Sant'Apollinare Nuovo). To early Christian communities the arrival of the Magi in Bethlehem assured Gentiles of a place in the New Covenant, hence this sixth-century mosaic representation of the Magi wearing the fashionable trousers of barbarian Goths.

FUMIA   +SCS BALTHASSAR +SCS MELCHIOR +SCS GASPAR.

victim of a court plot to concentrate power in the hands of Haakon, and was murdered on the island of Egilsay on April 16, 1116. The *Orkneyinga Saga* relates that Magnus instructed Haakon's cook, Lifolf, to "hew on my head a great wound, for it is not seemly to behead chiefs like thieves. Take good heart, poor wretch, for I have prayed to God for thee, that he be merciful unto thee."

Although Magnus was certainly not killed for his faith, but rather as the result of Haakon's desire to remove a political rival, he was popularly venerated as a martyr. The body of Magnus was eventually removed to Kirkwall, where Earl Rognvald began work on a new cathedral to house his remains in 1137.

Mark *First century*

Evangelist Feast day April 25. Feast of the translation of relics January 31

Author of *St. Mark's Gospel*, Mark is identified by most scholars with John Mark, the son of Mary, whose house was used by the apostles in Jerusalem. He may also be the young man who witnessed the arrest of Christ and fled naked to avoid capture. *Collosians* maintains that Mark was a cousin of Barnabas, which explains his inclusion in the first missionary journey of Paul and Bar-

nabas, but he returned to Jerusalem from Perga (Pamphylia), prompting Paul to refuse him a place on a second journey:

> But Paul thought [it] not good to take with them [Mark] who departed from them from Pamphylia, and went not with them to the work. And the contention was so sharp between them, that they departed asunder one from the other; and so Barnabas took Mark, and sailed unto Cyprus (*Acts* 15[38-39]).

Paul's *Captivity Epistles* make it clear that the two were later reconciled. Peter also refers to Mark as "my son" in a letter generally believed to have been written from Rome.

According to Papias, Bishop of Hierapolis, writing about 120, Mark's gospel was based on the testimony of Peter, and though modern scholars believe that Mark also made use of other witnesses, most agree that the gospel was written in Rome. Some things can be adduced about Mark from the New Testament – that he was Jewish but well-traveled; familiar with the Gentile customs of Rome; spoke Aramaic and probably Latin, in addition to Koiné, the dialect of Greek spoken throughout the eastern Mediterranean and in which he wrote his gospel – but nothing more is reliably known. The tradition that he traveled to Alexandria from Rome is recorded by Eusebius of Caesarea in the early fourth century

LEFT: *St. Mark Frees a Slave*, engraving of 1870 based on the painting by Jacopo Tintoretto. The daring foreshortening of Tintoretto's brilliant 1548 canvas made his reputation, and led to his being commissioned to produce a series of paintings of the miracles of St. Mark for the Republic of Venice.

RIGHT ABOVE: *St. Mark Rescues a Saracen*, by Jacopo Tintoretto. As patron of a maritime city, Venice, St. Mark's abilities to save those in peril at sea were highly valued, a counterpart to the activities of St. Nicholas down the Adriatic coast in Bari. Tintoretto's painting of *c*.1570 shows just such an event, as well as stressing his patronage of those who were enslaved, as St. Mark frees a young Saracen from a slaving ship in distress.

but, significantly, there is no mention of Mark in the writings of the great second-century Alexandrian theologians. Eusebius' claim subsequently hardened into the belief that he was Alexandria's founding bishop, and was martyred there. The Venetians certainly believed this, and it inspired the "recovery" of the relics of St. Mark from Alexandria in 828, and the founding of the church of San Marco by Doge Giustiniano Participazio. The accounts of the life and posthumous miracles of St. Mark which circulated during the Middle Ages are exclusively Venetian compositions, and formed the textual basis for the magnificent series of mosaics of his life surviving in the present, eleventh-century, basilica of San Marco. The use of a lion to symbolize St.

Mark is due to Jerome's *Prologue to the Gospels*, in which the lion, creature of the desert, is equated with the "voice of one crying in the wilderness," one of the phrases with which Mark opens his gospel.

Martha *First century*
Sister of Mary and Lazarus
Feast day July 29

According to John, Martha was the sister of Mary and Lazarus of Bethany. She rebuked Jesus for not having hurried to the side of Lazarus while he was ill, and her faith prompted his declaration "I am the resurrection and the life." Her confession, "I believe that thou art the Christ, the Son of God, which should come into the world," was the prelude to the miracle of the resurrection of Lazarus. Luke relates the story of Martha preparing the meal while her sister, Mary, sat listening to Christ:

But Martha was cumbered about with much serving, and came to him and said, Lord, dost thou not care that my sister hath left me to serve alone? Bid her therefore that she help me. And Jesus answered and said unto her, Martha, Martha, thou art careful and troubled about many things: But one thing is needful. Mary hath chosen that good part, which shall not be taken away from her.

Medieval theologians considered that this passage demonstrated the primacy of the *Vita Contemplativa* (Mary) over the *Vita Activa* (Martha), and Martha became increasingly identified with housekeepers and lay sisters, her standard attributes being a ladle, a broom and a set of keys. The discovery of her supposed relics at Tarascon (Provence) in 1187 is connected with the cult of Lazarus and Mary Magdalen in both Provence and Burgundy, but was the occasion for the one great legend which takes her away from this domestic role. For it was believed she had tamed a dragon by sprinkling it with holy water, before leading it to Arles with a sash tied around its neck, where it was killed.

Martin of Tours *c.316-97*
Bishop Feast day November 11.
Feast of the translation of relics July 4

Born in the Roman province of Pannonia (Hungary) and raised in Pavia (Lombardy), Martin was the son of a professional officer in the Roman army, and despite his father's paganism seems to have become a catechumen at an early age. Martin also served in the army, possibly as a conscript, but in about 350 demanded a discharge on the grounds of conscience; his biographer, Sulpicius Severus, maintained that he used the words: "I am a soldier of Christ. I am not allowed to fight." This stand was motivated by Martin's encounter with a beggar in Amiens, whose near-naked frame he clothed with half his cloak, a gesture which was followed by a dream in which Christ appeared wearing the cloak he had surrendered. The manner in which his life unfolded following this is uncertain. It seems that, after a period of imprisonment, his release from the army was approved, and he joined the brilliant Neoplatonist convert Hilary at Poitiers, where he was baptized. After this he traveled extensively in Lombardy, Dalmatia, Pannonia and Liguria. Although it is plausible that Martin only left Poitiers after Hilary was exiled at the Synod of Bitterae in 356, the early accounts suggest his journeys began with a visit to his parents shortly after his baptism.

ABOVE: *St. Martha*, seventeenth-century engraving. Martha is here seen not as the redoubtable tamer of dragons, but as a protector of servants and housemaids.

LEFT: *Investiture of St. Martin* (Simone Martini: Assisi, Lower Church of San Francesco). Simone Martini's fresco of c.1320 forms part of a cycle devoted to the life of St. Martin, in a chapel which is also dedicated to the saint. The scene is derived from an apocryphal medieval life, and shows St. Martin knighted by the Emperor Julian, before his renunciation of the sword.

On Hilary's return from exile in Phrygia, Martin joined him in Poitiers, and shortly after 360 founded a monastery in a "desert" at Ligugé (Poitou: all early monasteries were described as "deserts," a reflection of their origins in the third-century eremitical communities of the Syrian and Egyptian deserts). Disciples soon began to join him in what is widely regarded as the first monastery to take root in Gaul, although it would be a mistake to see too close a parallel between these early eremitical communities and "Benedictine" monasticism. They did not require stability of residence, and Ligugé served Martin as a base from which to begin a series of missionary journeys. He seems to have moved north into the Touraine in the late 360s, and was acclaimed Bishop of Tours c.372, by popular consent. On taking up his appointment Martin continued to live as an ascetic, initially in a cell by the cathedral, later at the great monastery he established in the "desert" at Marmoutier, some two miles north-east of Gallo-Roman Tours. His episcopate proved influential, for his tireless missionary journeys covered the whole of his vast diocese, and were responsible not only for the emergence of a rudimentary system of rural parishes, a wholly new initiative in Gaul, but equally for the development of the principle of episcopal "visitation" of outlying centers. His reputation as a living saint was also reinforced by reports of his ability to heal the sick.

Martin eventually died at Candes (Touraine) on November 8, 397, and the monks of Marmoutier beat those of Ligugé in the race for his body. The story then goes that some three days later, as the monks approached Tours along the Loire, the winter trees turned to leaf, birds sang, and a carpet of flowers settled along the banks. Martin was interred on November 11 in an established Christian cemetery about one mile west of the walled city of Tours, and by the mid-430s miracles began to be reported at the site. These seem to have acted as a pretext for the decision of St. Brice to build a modest chapel above Martin's grave, which was swiftly replaced under Bishop Perpet by a sumptuous funerary basilica – "large and magnificent, where one might count 8 doors, 52 windows and 120 columns" – St. Martin was translated to a new marble sarcophagus on July 4, 470.

The effect of the cult of St. Martin on early medieval France, indeed early Christendom, was considerable. In the first place,

the *Vita* composed by Martin's great friend and companion in later life, Sulpicius Severus, was regarded as a model life by later hagiographers. Secondly, Martin's was the first genuinely popular cult which was not centered on a martyr or New Testament figure. And thirdly, in 496 Clovis, King of the Franks, visited the shrine and promised to be baptized if he defeated the Alamanni. His Catholic baptism later that year in Reims gave him the excuse to move against Alaric II, the Arian King of the Visigoths, whose army he defeated at the battle of Vouillé in 507. These victories were associated with St. Martin, and seem to mark the beginning of a special relationship between Martin and the Merovingian monarchy, in which the saint was seen as the special protector and patron of the Franks.

Mary the Blessed Virgin
First century
Mother of Jesus Christ
Greatest feast day August 15

Known as Miriam in Hebrew, Mary is traditionally thought to be of the house of David, although the genealogies of Christ in *Matthew* and *Luke* trace the line through Joseph. The gospels make no mention of her early life, and when Mary is first introduced by St. Luke she is a "virgin espoused to a man whose name was Joseph," and is living in Nazareth. Both Mat-

thew and Luke recount the story of how the angel Gabriel appeared to her, and announced that by the power of the Holy Spirit she would conceive and bear a son "who shall be great, and shall be called the Son of Highest." Accepting that "with God, nothing shall be impossible," Mary replied, "Behold the handmaid of the Lord; be it unto me according to thy word" (*Luke* 1$^{37-38}$). Mary then visited her cousin, Elizabeth, who greeted her thus: "Blessed art thou among women, and blessed is the fruit of thy womb!" And Mary said "My soul doth magnify the Lord, and my spirit hath rejoiced in God my Savior" (*Luke* 1$^{42-47}$).

Mary features prominently in the narratives of the infancy of Christ, but is rarely mentioned in the accounts of Christ's ministry, appearing only in one of the sermons and at the wedding feast in Cana. She does, however, resurface at a significant point in John's Gospel, where we are told:

There stood by the cross of Jesus his mother. . . . When Jesus therefore saw his mother, and the disciple standing by, whom he loved [John], he saith unto his mother 'Woman, behold thy son!' Then saith he to the disciple 'Behold thy mother!' And from that hour the disciple took her into his own home (*John* 19$^{25-27}$).

After the Ascension of Christ, Mary was with the apostles in the upper room when they were filled with the Holy Spirit at Pentecost, and then she disappears from the narrative of *Acts of the Apostles*. None of the New

FAR LEFT ABOVE: St. Martin dividing his cloak to give to a beggar, detail from an altarpiece of *c.*1440 by the Sienese painter Stefano Sassetta.

FAR LEFT BELOW: *St. Martin Dividing his Cloak*, engraving by the fifteenth-century artist Martin Schongauer.

LEFT: The Dormition and Assumption of the Virgin Mary (Strasbourg Cathedral, south transept portal). Attitudes to the death and bodily assumption of the Virgin Mary differed between the Eastern and Western Churches; although both agreed that the body ascended to heaven, there was disagreement over when the soul preceded it. The iconography of this tympanum of *c.*1230 at Strasbourg is derived from Byzantium, and shows the body of the Virgin laid out upon a bed, and Christ holding her soul.

Testament epistles make any mention of Mary, and nothing is known of her later life, although, from an early date, both Ephesus and Jerusalem were claimed to be the place of her death.

Enormous significance came to be attached to Mary's role in the redemption of mankind, and both the Greek and Latin Churches devoted much theological effort to clarifying her position. Justin Martyr, the second-century Roman writer, saw Mary as the "New Eve," arguing that her obedience to God displaced the disobedience of Eve, while the notion of her perpetual virginity was first propounded as early as the mid-second century, featuring in the apocryphal *Book of James*. The main strands of theolog-ical opinion were eventually settled at the 431 Council of Ephesus, when the title of *Theotokos*, Mother of God, was formally be-stowed on Mary. In the West, **Ambrose** had also identified her as a type for the Church, *Ecclesia*, and with the doctrine of her bodily assumption into Heaven formulated by Gregory of Tours in the late sixth century, the principal beliefs of the Middle Ages had been established.

The medieval contribution to the cult of Mary is mostly legendary, the exception being the doctrine of the Immaculate Con-ception. This probably first took shape in the eastern Mediterranean during the seventh century and asserts that, as Mary is entirely without sin, she was protected by

LEFT: *Pietà* (Michelangelo: Vatican, St. Peter). The image of the Virgin Mary holding the body of the crucified Christ was one of a number of new compositional types which first found favor during the thirteenth century, all designed to help the viewer empathize with the suffering of Mary or Christ. Michelangelo's youthful version of the composition was probably completed c.1499, and in its avoidance of any extremes of gesture perhaps involves the viewer more closely in the contemplation of grief.

God from the very moment of conception in her mother's womb. The doctrine was particularly popular in late Anglo-Saxon England, where Eadmer of Canterbury wrote a treatise in its defence, but it was a matter of theological dispute throughout the Middle Ages, and **Bernard of Clairvaux**, **Thomas Aquinas** and the Dominicans all opposed it.

The legendary accounts of Mary's life are legion, and mostly concentrate on her early life. The most important are the apocryphal *Gospel of the Birth of the Virgin*, and a compilation of the *Miracles of the Blessed Virgin* assembled by William of Malmesbury and others at the beginning of the twelfth century. The apocryphal gospel represents her as the daughter of Anna and Joachim, saying that she was brought up in the Temple of Jerusalem, where she was responsible for weaving the priests' robes, and

makes much of her betrothal to Joseph. It was understandably popular, and its vivid narrative style lent itself to illustration; Giotto's account of the early life of the Virgin in the Arena Chapel, Padua, is perhaps the best known. Even Jacopo da Voragine, in his *Golden Legend*, found little reason to further embellish the tales, and his text is lifted almost verbatim from the *Gospel of the Birth of the Virgin*.

By contrast, the miracle stories all stress the intercessionary powers of Mary, her help in saving sinners, her compassion, and her advocacy of the plight of the meek and despairing when faced with the terror of Divine Judgment. This latter role, Mary as compassionate intercessor, is the main driving force behind the growth of the cult of the Virgin during the Middle Ages. The appearance of a number of Marian relics during the early Middle Ages certainly

ABOVE: *The Annunciation* by Simone Martini and Lippo Memmi. This expressive altarpiece was one of four concerned with the life of the Virgin which originally embellished the transepts of Siena Cathedral, and carries a date, 1333. What differentiates it from most early fourteenth-century Annunciations is its particularity. The text "Hail, thou art highly favored, the Lord is with thee" is tooled into the gold ground separating the angel from Mary, while Mary shies away; this is an Annunciation of disquiet.

helped the spread of the cult – the tunic worn by Mary at the birth of Christ (Chartres), a vial containing milk from the Virgin's breast (Walsingham), her wedding-ring (Cunault), and the girdle she was supposed to have given to the Apostle Thomas at her Assumption (three were claimed, at Prato Cathedral, Le Puy-Notre-Dame, and Westminster Abbey, respectively) – but the cult developed most rapidly between the twelfth and fourteenth centuries. The principal Marian feasts are the Purification (February 2), Annunciation (March 25), Visitation (July 2), Assumption (August 15), Nativity (September 8), Presentation (November 21), and Conception (December 8).

Mary Magdalen
First century
Patron of penitent sinners
Feast day July 22

One of the "women who had been healed of evil spirits and infirmities," Mary followed Christ in Galilee, and Luke says that Christ cast seven devils out of her. Mark records she was present at the Crucifixion and that "when the sabbath was past, Mary Magdalen, and Mary the mother of James, and Salome, had brought sweet spices, that they might come and annoint him." Matthew and John also maintain that she was the first to whom the risen Christ appeared:

She, supposing him to be the gardener, saith unto him, Sir, if thou have borne him hence, tell me where thou hast laid him, and I will take him away. Jesus saith unto her, Mary. She turned herself and saith unto him Rabboni; which is to say, Master. Jesus saith unto her, Touch me not, for I am not yet ascended to my Father; but go to my brethren and say unto them, I ascend unto my Father, and your Father; and to my God and your God.

In the Latin Church Mary Magdalen was identified with the "woman who was a sinner" who annointed Christ's feet in the house of Simon and with Mary, the sister of Martha and Lazarus. This identification was never accepted in the East and has now been rejected by the Roman Catholic Church, but it was popular in the West from an early date and, following its endorsement by **Gregory the Great**, it enjoyed general acceptance. It also forms a vital link between the biblical narratives and the later development of her cult, for it was on this basis alone that Mary Magdalen was revered

LEFT: *Mary Magdalen* by Rogier van der Weyden. This panel showing the Magdalen holding a pot of anointing oil forms the left-hand panel of a triptych of *c.*1440. The gesture of lamentation is directed toward the central panel, in which the Virgin and St. John are seen at the base of the cross.

RIGHT: La Madeleine, Vézelay, view of the nave looking east. Vézelay was the great twelfth-century cult center of the Magdalen, and one of the major pilgrimage churches of Romanesque and early Gothic France. The contrast between the early twelfth-century nave, part of the *ecclesia peregrinorum* consecrated in 1132, and the late twelfth-century choir, explicitly modeled on that of St-Denis, is intentionally dramatic, and among the most memorable of any pilgrimage center of medieval Europe.

as the savior of repentant sinners and as the supreme example of the contemplative woman.

This cult was the focus of one of the most celebrated cases of disputed ownership of the Middle Ages. The Eastern tradition holds that in later life Mary Magdalen joined John at Ephesus, where she died and was buried. The Anglo-Saxon evangelist and pilgrim St. Willibald told his biographer, Hugeburc, that he had been shown the tomb at Ephesus during the 720s, well before its translation to Constantinople at the very end of the ninth century. The Western tradition conflates the story of the Magdalen's later life with that of **Lazarus**, said to have been cast adrift in a leaky boat by hostile Jews, and then changes the destination from Cyprus to Provence. According to this legend, Mary Magdalen, Lazarus and **Martha** were placed in a boat with neither oars nor rudder, and fetched up on the coast of Provence, where they converted many to Christianity before the Magdalen died and was buried at St-Maximin. The story is first heard in the late eighth century and, improbable though it seems, formed the basis for two competing claims.

The shrine of Mary Magdalen in the crypt of La Madeleine at Vézelay was one of the great pilgrimage destinations of medieval western Europe, and its church is regarded by many as one of the finest essays in popular devotional imagery ever to grace France. What is most surprising about this status is that the earliest mention of Mary Magdalen at Vézelay is no earlier than about 1040. The eleventh-century accounts maintain that a monk by the name of Badilon had removed the relics of the Magdalen from the church of St-Maximin (near Aix-en-Provence), and brought them to Vézelay for safekeeping. These claims were far from universally

accepted, but nonetheless the Cluniac monastery SS Peter, Paul and Mary was re-dedicated to La Madeleine in 1050, and Vézelay's stock began to rise. By the late eleventh century a major pilgrimage was underway and in 1096, with money doubtless pouring into the offertory boxes, Abbot Artaud took the decision to rebuild the church. This building campaign was not without problems. Norgaud, Bishop of Autun, forbade all contributions at the

ABOVE: *Noli Me Tangere*, engraving by Anton Wierieux of an original by Martin de Vos. The text here is taken from St. John's gospel, where Mary Magdalen mistook Christ for a gardener.

LEFT: Mary Magdalen anoints the feet of Christ, early fifth-century ivory panel from Rome.

RIGHT ABOVE: *St. Matthew*, fifteenth-century Byzantine icon.

shrine of the Magdalen in 1100 – the monks' revenge came in 1103, when Pope Pascal II confirmed their spurious claim to the relics of Lazarus, otherwise claimed by Autun – and a fire in 1120 caused considerable damage to the fabric. When the *ecclesia peregrinorum* (pilgrims' church) was finally consecrated in 1132, however, it could justly claim to be among the most commodious in all Gaul.

Despite an enquiry into the authenticity of the relics under Pope Eugenius III in 1151, Vézelay continued to attract immense numbers of pilgrims, a situation which continued well into the thirteenth century. In 1279, however, disaster struck. The monks of St-Maximin revealed recently-discovered documents which described the concealment of the relics of the Magdalen for fear of damage during ninth-century Saracen raids, and Pope Boniface VIII accepted the Provençal claims. Thereafter Vézelay declined and St-Maximin became the center of the cult of the Magdalen, although in truth its popularity in Provence never vied with the great days of the twelfth century. The nature of the dispute lessened belief in the authenticity of either set of relics, and the late medieval cult of the Magdalen was more concerned with the exemplary nature of Mary as Christ's servant, than with the healing nature of her relics.

Matthew *First century*
Apostle and evangelist
Feast day September 21

"And as Jesus passed forth from thence, he saw a man, named Matthew, sitting at the receipt of custom: and he saith unto him, Follow me. And he arose, and followed him" (*Matthew* 9[9]). A later passage in Matthew's gospel identifies him as a Jew who worked for the Roman authorities as a tax-collector. Both Mark and Luke refer to him as Levi, but by whichever name, he is mentioned in all New Testament lists of the apostles.

The tradition that Matthew the Apostle also wrote the first gospel is early but problematical. Papias, writing around 120, maintains that Matthew composed an anthology of Christ's sayings in Hebrew, while Irenaeus (*c.*130-*c.*200) refers to the gospel as written by Matthew. Thereafter, the attribution was universally accepted. Most biblical scholars believe the gospel to have been written between *c.*70 and *c.*100 AD, but as it makes use of "Q" (a presumed collection of the sayings of Christ common to Matthew

LEFT: *St. Matthew*, Lindisfarne Gospels. This full-page portrait of Matthew as Evangelist precedes the gospel text and was painted in Northumbria between 687 and 698. It is modeled on a Mediterranean author portrait.

and Luke), which was written in Greek, Papias' "Hebrew" anthology cannot refer to the gospel. The accounts of Matthew's martyrdom are all far later, the *Roman Martyrology* insisting he died in Ethiopia while the *Hieronymianum* (a list of martyrs compiled in mid-fifth-century Italy, claiming, falsely, to be by Jerome) gives Tarrium in Persia as the place of death. The symbol of Matthew the Evangelist, a winged man, is again derived from Jerome's argument in the *Prologue to the Gospels* that, as the gospel opens with the *Liber Generationis*, a genealogical table, Matthew stresses the human.

Michael
Archangel Feast day September 29

Michael appears in the Old Testament as "the great prince which standeth for the children of thy people" (*Daniel* 12^1), and in the *Epistle of Jude* as the archangel who rebuked the devil about the body of Moses. He is best known for the part he played in the Fall of the Rebel Angels:

And there was war in heaven; Michael and his angels fought against the dragon; and the dragon fought and his angels. And prevailed not; neither was their place found any more in heaven. And the great dragon was cast out, that old serpent, called the Devil, and Satan, which deceiveth the whole world; he was cast out into the earth (*Revelation* 12$^{7-9}$).

The battle was recounted by John Milton in *Paradise Lost*. Michael also features in a number of apocryphal texts, notably the second- to fourth-century *Ascension of Isaiah*, where he is described as "the great captain, who is set over the best part of mankind." Several other early apocryphal writings mention his power to rescue and judge souls, which presumably lie behind the medieval view that, come the Last Judgment, Michael would hold the scales for the weighing of souls.

Constantine encouraged the growth of the cult in the eastern Mediterranean, dedicating a church and hospital to Michael at Sosthenion, outside Constantinople. Here he was regarded as the special protector of the sick. In the West the cult took on a very different character, for complex reasons perhaps best explained in terms of human psychology and pagan displacement. The earliest great sanctuary in the West was at Monte Gargano (southern Italy), where, on May 8, 492, the Archangel Michael appeared in a vision to Lawrence, Bishop of Siponto,

instructing him to dedicate a grotto to Christian worship at the very top of the mountain. According to tradition this was consecrated by Michael himself. Prior to its Christianization, Monte Gargano had been a significant Mithraic center, and the Mithraic emblem of a god plunging a sword into the neck of a bull has obvious parallels with the apocalyptic image of St. Michael killing the dragon with a sword or spear. Furthermore, Mithraism was basically a late Roman army cult, and Michael's victory in the "war in heaven" and his identification as "the great captain" had already led to his adoption as a protector of soldiers. Add to this the understandable association between angels and high places, and you have most of the ingredients of the medieval cult in the West.

Michael as a patron of high places is a theme encountered throughout the medie-

ABOVE: *St. Matthew*, Book of Kells. Pictured before an apse semidome, and caught within a border of animal interlace, the Kells' St. Matthew may well have been intended to mesmerize the viewer.

val West. It became the custom to dedicate upper chapels to Michael, for instance, something frequently seen at the west end of churches, while a number of isolated rocks off the coast of north-western Europe gained dedications to Michael between the eighth and twelfth centuries, as at Skellig Michael (Kerry), or St. Michael's Mount (Cornwall). The most spectacular of these islands is Mont-St-Michel (Manche), and the story of its legendary foundation contained in the late-tenth-century *Revelatio Ecclesiae Sancti Michaelis* soon entered the medieval canon. According to this, the Archangel Michael appeared one night in 708 to Aubert, Bishop of Avranches, instructing the bishop to build a church in his honor on Mont Tombe (the earlier name given to the

124

outcrop). Aubert convinced himself this was a dream, rather than a divinely ordained apparition, and Michael had to appear three times before his wishes were taken seriously, finally scorching a hole in Aubert's skull with the radiance of his indicative finger. Aubert took the last message at face value and founded an oratory on the rock, consecrated in 709 and staffed by canons, several of whom were sent to Monte Gargano to obtain relics associated with St. Michael. Whatever the merits of this account, it is certainly the case that Mont-St-Michel was attracting a pilgrimage by 867, when we hear of a certain Bernard who had traveled to "Jerusalem, Rome, Monte Gargano, and St-Michel-aux-Deux-Tombes" [modern Mont-St-Michel]. And with the canons replaced by Benedictine monks in 967, northern Europe had acquired one of its great pilgrimage centers.

Millán de la Cogolla
473-574?
Hermit Feast day November 12

A *cogolla* is a hood (literally translated as cowl), and Millán's is perhaps the greatest monastic cult of early medieval Spain. According to Braulio of Zaragoza's early seventh-century *Vita*, Millán was born at Berceo (La Rioja, Spain), and spent his youth working as a shepherd in the hills above the Cárdenas valley. Entranced by the music of a zither he used to play to entertain the sheep, he retired to live in a small cave above the river some time in the early sixth century. The Bishop of Tarazona saw in this a sign of holiness and entrusted Millán with the parish of Berceo, but he immediately distributed the parish funds to the poor and the cathedral clergy threw him out. Braulio maintains he lived to the age of 101, astonishing all with the speed and prodigality with which he performed miracles, turning invaders back from city gates, restoring sight to the blind, and expelling demons from the afflicted.

The *Vita* has a breathless and legendary tone throughout and is mostly pious fiction, but a popularly venerated hermit undoubtedly did live in the Cárdenas cave. The site attracted a community of monks by the 630s at the latest, and was refounded as the monastery of San Millán de Suso in 923, whose Mozarabic monks established one of the more important monastic scriptoria of early medieval Spain.

Nicholas *Fourth century?*
Bishop Feast day December 6.
Feast of the translation of relics May 9

Despite the enormous popularity of the cult of St. Nicholas in both the Eastern and Western Churches, the early documents are silent. That he was a fourth-century bishop of Myra, in Lycia (Turkey), seems well attested, but everything else is cultic. The earliest recorded dedication of a church to St. Nicholas is mid-sixth-century, but as this was a foundation of Justinian's in Constantinople, it probably signifies imperial approval of a devotion which had already taken root. Precisely when this interest was first felt is uncertain, but the archaeologists responsible for excavating the complex of churches on the island of Gemile (near Fethiye, south-western Turkey) in the early 1990s believe that this was where Nicholas

ABOVE: *St. Michael*, Shaftesbury Psalter. In this mid-twelfth-century English prefatory miniature, it is the promise of the Last Judgment which is stressed, with Michael carrying the souls of the blessed to Paradise.

RIGHT: St. Millán, Yuso, La Rioja, Spain. Superb late eleventh-century ivory plaque from the shrine of San Millán, showing Millán flanked by monks.

LEFT: *The Glorification of St. Nicholas* by Lorenzo Lotto. Lotto's 1529 altarpiece was painted for the nave chapel of St. Nicholas in the church of the Carmini, and depicts the saint in the full regalia of a bishop, in the company of SS John the Baptist and Lucy.

was initially buried during the fourth century. If so, he was placed in a rock-cut tomb in the island's highest church, and at the end of a processional way. Gemile was abandoned after it was threatened by an Arab fleet in the mid-seventh century, when it is thought the body of Nicholas was moved to the inland safety of Myra.

Things only began to take on a universal dimension after Methodius, Patriarch of Constantinople between 842 and 847, wrote a life of Nicholas, a text which became known in the West through a tenth-century Latin translation. Methodius' life is a brilliant web of pious fiction, guaranteed to attract a wide following by appealing to just about every disadvantaged group imaginable, and seems to have taken Europe by storm. The principal stories subsequently associated with Nicholas are all to be found here, mostly revolving around threes: the three sailors he saved from a tempest off the coast of Asia Minor; the three unjustly condemned men he released from prison; the three bags of gold he dropped through a poor man's window, to provide his daughters with a dowry and so save them from prostitution (the origin, incidentally, of the three golden balls which act as a pawnbroker's sign); and the three young boys he brought to life after they had been murdered in a brine-tub by an unscrupulous butcher. Sailors, prisoners, children and unmarried women – all began to see in Nicholas a protector.

The emergence of Bari (Apulia, Italy) as the center of the cult is the result of one of the most celebrated cases of reliquary theft of the Middle Ages. By the middle of the eleventh century, Lycia was in the hands of the Saracens and the tomb of Nicholas at Myra was thus technically under Moslem control, although the shrine itself was still served by a community of monks. Despite this latter fact, and partly motivated by news from Venice that the maritime community there was also planning a raid on Myra, 62 sailors in three ships set sail from Bari with the express intention of seizing the body. The raid was successful and on May 9, 1087, Elias, abbot of San Benedetto de Bari, received the relics of St. Nicholas on the quayside. Thereafter Elias began work on a new church to accommodate the saint, and two years later, while Pope Urban II was in Bari, the relics were translated into the crypt of the church of San Nicola.

The pilgrimage to the shrine of San Nicola at Bari was among the most prolific

ABOVE: St. Nicholas in prison, striking late thirteenth-century representation of Nicholas sharing the fate of the prisoners, of whom he was regarded as protector.

LEFT: St. Nicholas resurrects the boys in the brine-tub (Rouen, rue St-Romain). As a protector of children and prostitutes, images of St. Nicholas were frequently attached to the angle-posts of late medieval houses. This particular example dates from the late fifteenth-century, and borrows from a popular fourteenth-century version of the story, which situates the action in Athens and substitutes the two sons of a wealthy merchant for the three students of the earliest account.

of the Middle Ages, and served to further popularize an already popular saint. The number of churches dedicated to Nicholas in western Europe is testimony to this, as is the habit of giving presents to children on the feast of St. Nicholas (December 6), which seems first to have taken hold in the Netherlands during the fifteenth century. A Dutch dialect form of St. Nicholas, *Sinteklaas*, is the origin of Santa Claus, and as the tradition of gifts merged with ancient Norse winter rites in the Dutch colonies of North America, Santa Claus became Father Christmas.

Nicholas the Pilgrim
1075-94
Pilgrim Feast day June 2

A Greek youth, allegedly from Stiro, Nicholas vowed to undertake a pilgrimage to Rome, took ship to Ótranto and wandered up the Apulian coast. He traveled carrying a cross, his speech limited to the words *Kyrie Eleison* (Lord, have mercy), a cry which was taken up by the crowds of children who followed him. As he wound through Lecce, Bríndisi and Bari, he was taken for a lunatic and generally treated as an object of ridicule. He fell ill on reaching Trani, and died on the steps of the cathedral on June 2, 1094. Miracles were reported at the grave within days of his death, and in 1098 Bishop Bisantius took advantage of the gathering of prelates at the council of Bari to have the canonization of Nicholas the Pilgrim rushed through by Pope Urban II. Work on a new cathedral to accommodate the shrine of Nicholas the Pilgrim probably began in the same year, 1098, but it was a slow campaign and the relics were only translated into the crypt in 1143, when the cathedral was rededicated to San Nicola Pellegrino.

Nicholas the Pilgrim is a good example of a cult inspired by rivalry with a neighbor. In 1087, Elias of Bari had taken delivery of the relics of the great eastern Mediterranean miracle-worker, Nicholas of Myra (see **Nicholas**), and Bari was a mere 30 miles along the coast. Trani even seems to have played a part in the struggle for the possession of the relics of Nicholas of Myra after they had arrived. In a number of respects Nicholas the Pilgrim offers an interesting parallel with the later cult of William of Perth (died 1201) at Rochester. Like Rochester, on the road to the shrine of **Thomas Becket** at Canterbury, Trani lay on the route

to a major pilgrimage center, and grew to profit from its position. And although neither cult ever seriously compared with those of Canterbury and Bari, their proven miracle-working powers developed into significant subsidiary attractions.

Olaf *995-1030*
Martyr and patron saint of Norway
Feast day July 29

A son of the noted Norse chieftain Harold Grenske, Olaf converted to Christianity in Normandy. By 1013 he was in England, and supported Ethelred II against the invasion army of Swein Forkbeard, subsequently finding employment with Duke Richard II of Normandy in his 1016 campaign against Odo of Chartres. His military skills were also recognized back home, and after defeating Swein in a naval battle in 1016 he ascended to the throne of Norway. His

ABOVE: St. Nicholas offers three bags of gold to the dowerless daughters, in this seventeenth-century woodcut.

RIGHT: St. Olaf (York; St Olave, Marygate). York was an important tenth-century Viking city and Olaf sustained a strong following there well into the sixteenth century. This stained glass figure dates from *c*.1500 and forms part of the east window.

political methods have much in common with those of his tenth-century predecessor, Olaf Tryggvesson; both of them were happy to coerce the Norse into accepting Christianity and to use any means available to root out heathenism. Olaf was defeated in battle by Cnut in 1028, however, and forced to withdraw to Sweden. His attempt to regain the Norwegian throne during the unpopular reign of Swein, son of Cnut, met with disaster and at the battle of Stiklestad, on July 29, 1030, his army was annihilated and he himself killed.

Olaf was proclaimed a martyr almost immediately. Legends of his asceticism grew, and reports of the healing powers of the waters which flowed from his grave reached Grimkell, Bishop of Nidaros (Trondheim), prompting the good bishop to build a chapel over the site. On August 3, 1031, in a state of apparent incorruption, Olaf's body was solemnly translated into a shrine. The growth of the cult was equally rapid, and the feast was observed throughout most of Scandinavia by the end of the eleventh century, while the earlier chapel was expanded as the cathedral church of Trondheim during the 1180s. His feast is also common to a number of English calendars, and with over 40 ancient church dedications in Britain, concentrated in the older Viking areas, Olaf must be counted one of the more popular saints of medieval north-western Europe.

BELOW: Trani Cathedral. The bronze doors at Trani were designed by the local metalworker, Barisano de Trani, between 1175 and 1179. They depict, among other subjects, scenes from the life and miracles of St. Nicholas the Pilgrim.

Pantaleon *Died c.304?*

Martyr Feast day July 27

The name Pantaleon translates as "all-merciful," and although no early account of his life survives, the cult was popular in Bithynia (the region south and east of the sea of Marmara) from the fifth century onward. According to a late *Passio*, he was brought up a Christian by his mother, Eubula, but lapsed into paganism before being converted back into the Faith by a Christian named Hermalaos. His career as a medic led to his being appointed physician to the Emperor Galerius. He was denounced as a Christian during the persecution of Diocletian, and beheaded at Nicomedia in 304 or 305. He was widely venerated in the East as a healer and miracle-worker, and in the West as a patron of physicians. The Emperor Justinian was probably responsible for rebuilding his church at Nicomedia (Bithynia), while both Cologne and Ravello were important centers for his cult.

ABOVE: The west front of San Pantaleon, Cologne. As one of the main centers of the cult of San Pantaleon, Cologne acquired a church dedicated to the martyr under Archbishop Bruno, brother of the Emperor Otto II. Work began in 966 and the high altar was dedicated in 980, with the western choir added *c.*1000.

LEFT: *St. Pantaleon*, miniature from a twelfth-century Cologne gospel book. St. Pantaleon was rumored to be particularly helpful to those suffering from headaches.

Patrick *c.390-c.461*
Apostle of the Irish Feast day March 17

Patrick was born to a Christian Romano-British family who owned property at Bannavem Taburniae (site unidentified, but probably in western England or south-west Scotland). His father, Calpurnius, was a deacon in the Church. According to his own *Confessio*, written in Ireland toward the end of his life, Patrick was enslaved by Irish pirates at the age of 16 and set to work as a herdsman at "Foclut," probably in County Mayo. After six years of servitude he escaped, managed to make his way to a distant port and took ship to a "foreign land." The sequence of events from here is unclear and the subject of much scholarly controversy, but it seems Patrick was trained for the priesthood, returned to his family, and at some point in the early 430s was sent to Ireland as a missionary bishop. A number of discordant traditions about this period developed in the seventh century, many of them recorded in the *Book of Armagh*, according to which he was trained as a monk either at Lérins (Provence) or by **Germanus** at Auxerre (Burgundy). Britain is more likely, although Patrick probably did visit Gaul, and his training was a cause of considerable regret to him in his later life, when he bewailed how unlearned and intellectually ill-equipped he was.

Patrick must have arrived in Ireland shortly after Palladius had left. Palladius was originally sent by Pope Celestine I (422-31) as first Bishop of Ireland and worked in Wicklow, but he found few followers and retired to Scotland where, it is thought, he died. Patrick was probably appointed bishop as Palladius' successor, some time before 435, and established himself in the north, preaching, persuading local chieftains to entrust him with the education of their sons, and baptizing the newly converted. He founded the bishopric of Armagh, which he used as a base for his missionary journeys, and began to organize the Irish Church on the same diocesan principles as obtained in the surviving Roman Empire. It was an extremely successful mission and resulted in the foundation of the earliest monastic communities of monks or nuns in Ireland, as well as a system of suffragan bishoprics, but it was not without problems. He was constantly under threat from chieftains suspicious of the erosion of their authority, and encountered opposition from what appears to be a significant faction

LEFT: *The Devil Tempting St. Patrick* (Parisian engraving of 1530). Like many an early Christian saint, Patrick was prone to visitations from demons and tempters.

BELOW: *St. Patrick*, St. Patrick's Cathedral, New York. Neo-Gothic statue of Patrick as bishop and proselytizer.

within the Church, who saw him as a barely educated halfwit. He addresses this latter charge quite specifically in his *Confessio*, and with great modesty and dignity announces his personal *credo*: "I, Patrick, a sinner, am the most ignorant . . . among the faithful. I owe it to God's Grace that so many people should be born again to him through me."

Only one other text by St. Patrick survives, a letter to the British chieftain Coroticus, protesting about the attacks of British slavers on the Christian congregations of Ireland, and both his date and place of death are unknown. Early in the 460s seems the likely date, but as he was not buried at Armagh, disputes as to the ownership of his relics arose during the Middle Ages. Downpatrick was the most favored candidate, but there were other contenders, and even Glastonbury (Somerset) put forward a claim. The later stories of Patrick expelling the snakes from Ireland, or silencing the druids on the hill of Slane and confronting Laoghaire, "High King of Ireland," are legendary accretions and do not form part of his *Confessio*. Nonetheless the story of the snakes, and of Patrick expounding the nature of the Trinity by comparing it to a shamrock, gave rise to the most popular visualization of St. Patrick, as a preacher surrounded by snakes and shamrock.

Paul *Died c.65* AD
Apostle of the Gentiles.
Feast day June 29

Born at Tarsus in Cilicia to a Jewish family of the tribe of Benjamin, Paul was given the name Saul and raised as a Pharisee, receiving instruction from the renowned Rabbi Gamaliel in Jerusalem. Saul was among the early persecutors of Christianity, guarding the clothes of those who stoned **Stephen** and making "havoc of the church, entering into every house, and hailing men and women [committing] them to prison" (*Acts* 8[3]). It was while he was on his way to

LEFT: St. Paul lowered from the walls of the city of Damascus (Palermo, Capella Palatina), detail from the brilliant mosaics in Roger II's mid-twelfth-century court chapel.

RIGHT: *St. Paul at Ephesus*. Gustave Doré's mid-nineteenth-century engraving represents the burning of the books "of the men which used curious arts" at Ephesus. Having confessed their misdeeds to Paul, they were converted to Christianity.

Damascus to arrest more Christians that he underwent his famous conversion, the story being repeated three times in *Acts of the Apostles*. According to these Saul saw a great light and heard the words:

Saul, Saul, why persecutest thou me? And he said, Who art thou, Lord? And the Lord said, I am Jesus whom thou persecutest: it is hard for thee to kick against the pricks. Arise, and go into the city, and it shall be told thee what thou must do (*Acts* 9^4-6^).

He was baptized by Ananias and then retired to spend three years in solitude and prayer in Arabia. When he returned to Damascus, the Nabataean king, Aretas, was

so hostile that he had to be lowered in a basket from the city walls at the dead of night to make good his escape. He made his way to Jerusalem, where the Christian community was understandably cautious, and it was wholly due to the advocacy of the Apostle Barnabas that doubts were allayed and Saul accepted. Little is known about the period immediately after this, and it was several years later that Barnabas summoned Paul to Antioch, and along with **Mark** they set sail for Cyprus on the first missionary journey. During this voyage Barnabas seems to have ceded his position as leader to Saul, who is first referred to as Paul in *Acts of the*

BELOW: *St. Paul* (Ravenna, Arian Baptistry). In this mosaic of *c*.495, Paul is seen carrying the scrolls of the Law and leading a procession of the Apostles toward the *Crux Splendidior*, or jeweled cross, a reference perhaps to the silver-gilt cross which Theodosius II set up on Golgotha.

Apostles. Returning to Antioch *c.*49 AD, they gave an account of their work among the Gentiles and found themselves at odds with the Jewish Christian community, who maintained that without circumcision Gentiles could not be saved. In response, Paul and Barnabas traveled to Jerusalem to discuss the matter with **Peter** and the other apostles, a meeting usually described as the first Council of the Church, where their case was successful. The Mosaic Law was not to be imposed on non-Jews, and Paul's mission to the Gentiles was confirmed.

Paul was accompanied on his second missionary journey by Silas, founding a number of new churches in Asia Minor and Greece and preaching at Philippi, Thessalonica, Athens and Corinth, but his success was mixed and after 18 months he returned to Antioch. The third missionary journey was perhaps the most influential. He began by spending two years at Ephesus, working many miracles and winning large numbers of converts, in addition to writing his *First Letters to the Corinthians*. Driven from the city by rioting silversmiths, who feared their trade in silver offerings to the goddess Diana was under threat from the spread of Christianity, he continued to Macedonia and then Corinth, where he wrote his *Letter to the Romans*. He finally returned to Jerusalem in about 57 AD, where he was arrested and imprisoned for two years. His rights as a Roman citizen to a trial in Rome were eventually recognized, but as the prison ship went down off Malta, it was not until *c.*60 that he actually reached Rome itself. He was placed under house arrest for a further two years, during which time he wrote the four "Captivity Epistles" (*Philippians, Collosians, Philemon*, and *Ephesians*), and was probably acquitted, as a number of early texts refer to him revising Ephesus and traveling "to the limit of the Occident" (perhaps Spain?). *Acts of the Apostles* goes no further than to say he spent two years in captivity in Rome.

The late-second-century *Acts of Paul* offer much secondary information about Paul: that he was "short of stature, bald and bandy-legged;" and that he was beheaded during the persecution of Nero at a place subsequently known as Tre Fontane, along the left bank of the river Tiber and about three miles from the center of Rome. His body was taken for burial to a site just outside the city walls, over which Emperor Constantine built the church of San Paolo Fuori le Mura, magnificently rebuilt after

385 as a double-aisled basilica intended to rival that of St. Peter on the Vatican hill. His influence on Christian theology can scarcely be overstated. His views on Christ as the eternal Son of God, on the Church as the mystical body of Christ, and on the nature of grace, predestination and free will, and salvation, have permeated Christian thinking, and had a profound impact on the writings of **Augustine of Hippo**, **Thomas Aquinas** and Martin Luther.

Peter *Died c.64* AD
Apostle Feast day June 29

Originally called Simon and a native of Bethsaida, near the Sea of Tiberias, Peter was first introduced to Jesus by **Andrew**, his brother, and given the Aramaic name

Cephas, meaning rock (Peter is the English equivalent of the Greek for rock). This title was subsequently qualified when Jesus answered Peter's confession of faith with the words, "Thou art Peter, and upon this rock I will build my church; and the gates of hell shall not prevail against it. And I will give unto thee the keys of the kingdom of heaven." The story of Christ's calling Peter and Andrew to become "fishers of men" is related in all three synoptic gospels, while **Luke** adds that Peter and Andrew worked as fishermen in partnership with **James** and **John**, the sons of Zebedee. In all lists of the apostles, Peter is invariably named first.

Peter features prominently in the narratives of Christ's Ministry and Passion, and was part of an "inner group" with James and John, all of whom were privileged to witness the raising of Jairus' daughter, the Transfiguration, and the Agony in the Garden. Christ also asked him to share with John the preparations for the Last Supper. Shortly afterward, on the Mount of Olives, Peter assured Christ, "Though all men shall be offended because of thee, yet will I never be offended." Jesus said to him, "Verily I say unto thee, that this night, before the cock crow, thou shalt deny me thrice." Peter went on to deny all knowledge of Christ three times to the crowd which gathered around the house of Caiphas, the high priest, but was the first apostle to whom Christ appeared following the Resurrection, and at the breakfast by the Sea of Tiberias Christ charged Peter to "Feed my lambs. Feed my sheep."

After the Ascension of Christ, Peter was decisive in calling for the election of a twelfth apostle to replace Judas Iscariot, and was the first to perform a miracle "in the name of Jesus Christ of Nazareth." Thenceforth he acted as leader of the apostles, speaking before the Sanhedrin, passing

BELOW: *The Tribute Money* (Masaccio: Florence, Brancacci Chapel, Sta Maria del Carmine). Masaccio's fresco of *c*.1423-25 illustrates the famous story of Peter's payment of tribute money in Capernaum, when Christ asked Peter to "go to sea, and cast a hook, and take the fish that first cometh up; and when thou hast opened its mouth, thou shalt find a piece of money; that take, and give unto them for me and thee."

judgment on Ananias and Sapphira, and baptizing the first Gentile to be admitted into the Church, Cornelius the centurion. **Paul** sought his support at the Council of Jerusalem, and Peter's summing-up might be seen as the first clear exposition of the universal role of the Church. The later chapters of *Acts of the Apostles* make little mention of Peter, and although he is known to have visited Antioch and, quite possibly, Corinth (where a group professing loyalty to Cephas is mentioned by Paul), the evidence for the last years of his apostolate is circumstantial.

The *Epistle to the Corinthians* written by Clement of Rome *c.*96 AD mentions Peter's organization of the Church in Rome and his eventual martyrdom there under Nero *c.*64 AD. This is borne out by Ignatius of Antioch (Bishop of Antioch *c.*69 AD) and Irenaeus. The early traditions are all united on the point that Peter was crucified upside down at his own request, after Emperor Nero blamed the Christians for the great fire which devastated Rome in 64 AD. The tradition that Peter was buried on the Vatican hill is later, but the invocations scratched into the plaster on ancient walls around the

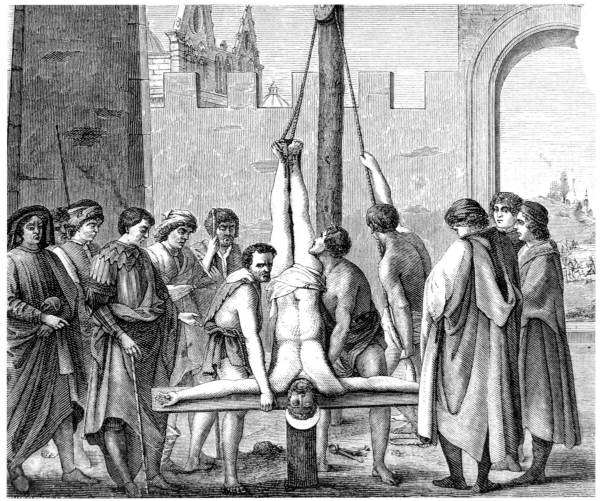

ABOVE LEFT: *St. Peter*, fourteenth-century Swedish stained glass window.

LEFT: *The Martyrdom of St. Peter*, engraving after a late fifteenth-century painting by Filippino Lippi. The tradition that Peter was crucified upside down at his own request is exceptionally early, and is quoted by the third-century Alexandrian theologian, Origen.

western end of the present church of the Vatican make it clear that by the mid-third century, at least, a memorial to Peter had been erected on the site. It is also significant that no other city has ever been suggested as the burial place of Peter.

By 319, the probable year that Constantine the Great began work on a new and splendid basilica over what was believed to be the tomb of St. Peter, a sizeable pilgrimage to the Vatican shrine had built up. Replaced during the sixteenth century, the Constantinian basilica is usually referred to as Old St. Peter's, and consisted of a large transept built out above the shrine of St. Peter, and a vast double-aisled nave which acted as a distinct funerary church. The relics were maintained beneath the apse, and prior to the building of a passage by **Gregory the Great** *c.*600, could only be seen by lifting a stone flag from the pavement and gazing down. The practice was to pray for intercession through this aperture, after which the supplicant presented a piece of cloth to one of the guardians. This was then weighed and lowered onto the tomb overnight. In the morning the cloth was hauled up and weighed again. If its weight had increased, the prayers would probably be answered.

Philibert *c.610-84*
Abbot Feast day August 20

Born in Gascony, Philibert was brought north by St. Ouen, who persuaded him to become a monk at his monastery of Rebais (Ile-de-France). Philibert was briefly abbot of Rebais, but his inability to control a turbulent and infractory body of monks led him to resign, and he followed St. Ouen into Normandy. It seems likely that he spent his early years in Normandy familiarizing himself with monastic practice in the new foundations then springing up in the northeast of the province, St-Wandrille perhaps among them. He put his knowledge to good use in 654, when he founded the abbey of Jumièges, on land donated by Clovis II above the right bank of the river Seine. He served Jumièges as abbot for 20 years, building three separate churches to serve the monks, but his denunciation of Ebroin, mayor of the Frankish palace, led to his imprisonment in Rouen in 674, and on his release he was exiled to the Poitou.

During his exile Philibert founded his second monastery, at Noirmoutier, an island close to the mouth of Loire, where he stayed until Ebroin's death in 681. With Noirmoutier successfully established, Philibert spent the last three years of his life encouraging the spread of monasticism in the Poitou, taking responsibility for the planting of new houses at Quincay, Luçon and Pavilly. It is a formidable list, comparable in its way with the earlier activities of **Martin of Tours**, or sixth- and seventh-century Irish missionaries such as Willibrord and Columbanus. And the attachment the monks felt to their founder offers a clear parallel with another major monastic saint. When Philibert died in 684 he was buried at Noirmoutier. The vulnerability of the island to the Norse raiding parties of the mid-ninth century, however, led the monks to carry the relics into exile, founding first St-Philibert-de-Grandlieu, *c.*851, then resting at Cunault (Anjou) between 858 and 862. When Norse ships began harrying the shores of the Loire as far east as Orléans, the monks again decamped, this time to St-Pourcain (Auvergne), before Charles the Bald gave them the abbey of St-Valérian at Tournus

BELOW: *St. Radegonde (Vita Radegundis)*. This miniature from an early twelfth-century copy of Venantius Fortunatus' *Life of St. Radegonde* shows Radegonde freeing prisoners from the garden at Péronne (top) and receiving thanks (bottom). The manuscript was probably illuminated in Poitiers and was intended for the edification of the community of the Holy Cross, Radegonde's own foundation.

(Burgundy) in 875, which was subsequently rededicated to St. Philibert. Their odyssey is akin to that of the congregation of **St. Cuthbert**, also driven by Viking raids, who carried the uncorrupted remains of their beloved patron from Lindisfarne to eventual peace at Durham.

Radegonde *c.518-87*
Queen and nun Feast day August 13

Daughter of Berthaire, King of Thuringia, contemporary accounts of Radegonde exist in the writings of Gregory of Tours and Venantius Fortunatus. She was captured by the Franks in about 531, and while in captivity converted to Christianity. The circumstances of her youth at the Frankish court are unclear but in about 540 she was coerced into marrying Clothaire, King of the Franks, and endured appalling treatment for the next six or seven years. Clothaire's assassination of her brother gave her the excuse to flee from court, and she took refuge in the household of Médard, Bishop of Noyon, who ordained her a deaconess around 549. After taking advice from a hermit, Jean, at Chinon, Radegonde resolved to found a nunnery at Poitiers, where she appointed one Agnes to act as abbess, and adopted the monastic Rule of Caesarius of Arles. Her success in persuading the Byzantine Emperor Justin II to send her a relic of the True Cross in about 569 inspired Venantius Fortunatus to write a famous hymn in her honor, *Vexilla Regis*, and inspired the dedication of the convent to the Holy Cross. Radegonde died surrounded by the nuns on August 13, 587.

Remigius *Died c.533*
Bishop In France more generally known as Remi. Feast day January 13. Feast of the translation of relics October 1

Although Remigius is mentioned by Gregory of Tours, the *Vita* traditionally attributed to the late-sixth-century poet Venantius Fortunatus is unlikely, in fact, to be sixth century, and the principal account of his life is contained in the *Vita* written by Hincmar of Reims during the mid-ninth century. As the latter has its own agenda and is mostly, if not entirely, fictional, the problems are formidable. That he was a bishop of Reims is undoubtedly true, and the most important episode associated with his life, his baptism of Clovis, certainly took place. Beyond that it is all conjecture. Remigius probably bap-

tized Clovis, the first Christian king of the Franks, in Reims Cathedral in the autumn of 496. Although he was married to a Christian, the Burgundian Clotilde, Clovis seems to have seen little advantage in his people's espousing Christianity before the mid-490s. When he did, in 496, it was after a visit to the shrine of **St. Martin** at Tours, when he promised to become baptized if he managed to defeat the Alamanni. This done, he redeemed his pledge.

The later significance of this baptism was considerable, for Clovis was one of the first Germanic tribal leaders to embrace Catholic, as opposed to Arian, Christianity, and it gave him the excuse to move against Alaric II, Arian king of the Visigoths, whose tribe he subsequently forced south of the Pyrenees. Secondly, it began an association

ABOVE: St-Remi, Reims, view of the choir looking east, showing Abbot Pierre de la Celle's breathtakingly luminous choir of *c.*1170-80.

between Reims and the Frankish monarchy which led to the kings of France receiving their crowns in Reims Cathedral. The *Vita* of Hincmar of Reims is principally responsible for the ceremonial link, since it claims that the holy oil Remigius used in the baptism of Clovis was miraculously brought to earth by a dove. This was self-replenishing, and contained within a precious casket, the *Sainte-Ampoulle*, which was lodged, along with the body of St. Remigius, in the great monastic church at Reims which bears his name, St-Remi. From the tenth century onward, this oil was used in the coronation of every monarch of France. The relics of St. Remigius were solemnly translated into a new shrine by Pope Leo IX on October 1, 1049.

Roch *Fourteenth century*
Plague saint Feast day August 16

Although Roch is undoubtedly a historical personality, there is considerable dispute as to the detail of his life, and even the dates at which he worked his many cures are uncertain. The standard account was written in Venice by Francesco Diedo in 1478, and

BELOW: *St. Roch* (Jacopo Tintoretto: Venice, Scuola Grande di San Rocco). Although the Venetian Confraternity of St. Roch was founded in 1478, Scarpagnino's new Scuola building was only completed *c.*1549. Tintoretto painted the interiors as the result of winning a competition in 1564, hence this image of *c.*1580.

makes use of several earlier traditions. According to this, Roch was born to a mercantile family in Montpellier (Languedoc), and was persuaded to live as a hermit and pilgrim by his father. While returning from a pilgrimage to Rome, he stopped at the plague-stricken town of Acquapendente (northern Lazio), where he cured many in the Sign of the Cross. He then traveled through northern Italy, and brought about similar recoveries from plague in Cesena, Mantua and Parma, before himself falling ill at Piacenza and retiring to the woods to die. His faithful dog refused to allow Roch to abandon himself in this way, and each day brought him a loaf of fresh bread. After his health returned, he made his way back to Montpellier, where his years on the road had so changed his appearance that he was arrested as a spy and sentenced to imprisonment, with his uncle acting as the presiding magistrate. He died in prison five years later. There the matter might have rested, but Francesco Diedo and others maintained that when the body was removed from the bed-board, the cell was filled with light, revealing the inscription, "All those who are stricken by plague and

BELOW: *The Feast Day of St. Roch* by Antonio Canaletto. Canaletto's early eighteenth-century portrayal shows the gathering outside the Scuola Grande di San Rocco in Venice, held each August to mark the feast of St. Roch.

LEFT: *The Martyrdom of St. Sebastian* by Antonio and Piero del Pollaiuolo. A desire to represent religious narrative in a way which was clear and memorable was always present in the medieval Church, but reached something of an apogee in fifteenth-century Italy. The Pollaiuolo brothers' vast altarpiece of 1475 was clearly intended as a vivid reminder of Sebastian's death.

pray for help through the intercession of Roch shall be healed."

Diedo's account is heavily embroidered, and precisely when Roch cured the sick is left open. The temptation is to see him at work during the Black Death of 1347-49 (at its most virulent in central Italy in the summer of 1348), but Roch is not mentioned in any of the contemporary chronicles, and it seems more likely he was in Italy during the secondary outbreaks of plague in 1363 or 1374. The cult developed in France and Italy in the fifteenth century, and by *c.*1430 Roch was routinely invoked whenever plague struck. In this respect the acquisition of his relics by Venice in 1485 is understandable, for there was no city in Europe more vulnerable to plague, more liable to import disease on her mercantile ships. The Scuola Grande di San Rocco, constructed between 1515 and 1549 and magnificently painted by Jacopo Tintoretto after 1564, and the adjacent church of San Rocco (1489), both just behind the Frari in Venice, became the focus for the actual reliquary cult as this developed in the sixteenth century.

Sebastian *Died c.304?*

Martyr Feast day January 20

According to a fifth-century *Acta*, Sebastian was born in Gaul and enlisted in the Roman army in about 283, rising to the position of captain in the Praetorian Guard under the Emperor Diocletian. On learning that Sebastian was a Christian, Diocletian ordered that he be taken to a place outside the city of Rome and shot with arrows. The archers presumed him dead, but he recovered after his wounds were tended by a Christian widow, Irene, and returned to rebuke Diocletian for his persecution of Christians. Diocletian then ordered him battered to death with clubs. This version of his life is pure invention, but it is likely that a Sebastian was martyred under Diocletian,

as his name appears in the list of Roman martyrs drawn up by the anonymous *Chronographer of 354*. The tradition that he was buried in a catacomb along the Via Appia is also early, though the great Constantinian funerary basilica which bears his name, San Sebastiano, was not originally built to house his cult.

His importance in the Middle Ages lies in his status as an intercessor against plague. The connection was made as early as the seventh century, but it was only during the Black Death of 1347-49 that Sebastian began to be invoked outside Rome, Ravenna or Milan. His identification as a plague saint was almost certainly due to the classical image of an angry god punishing humanity with disease-ridden darts, a role often taken by Apollo. Sebastian absorbed these arrows of pestilence on man's behalf and, with Roch, became, in the Latin West at least, the principal saint to whom those suffering from plague would turn.

Simeon the Stylite
c.390-459

Hermit Feast day September 1 in the East; January 5 in the West

Born to a shepherd family in Cilicia, Simeon entered the monastery at Eusebona (now Tell'Ada, Syria) while a youth, but was dismissed by the abbot for excessive self-mortification, and moved to Telanissos (now Qal'at Si'man, Syria) to live as an anchorite. His acts of penance and perceived holiness seem to have drawn visitors to Telanissos, anxious to draw strength from Simeon's extreme piety, and in about 423 he determined to escape the distractions of humankind by erecting a pillar on which he might live. The rest of his life was spent on top of various pillars, each one higher than the last, the fourth rising to 60 feet and acting as his home for the final 20 years of his life. At the top of this pillar was a platform of between six and twelve feet square, surrounded by a balustrade. Simeon would prostrate himself in prayer here, engaging in a total fast over Lent, and would address visitors twice daily.

Insofar as Simeon's motive was to avoid crowds the strategy failed, for huge numbers came to gawp at the spectacle of the pillar-dwelling hermit, the Emperors Theodosius and Marcian among them. His reported preaching is surprisingly benign, however, emphasizing the desirability of

FAR LEFT: *Simeon the Stylite*, sixteenth-century icon from Cyprus showing Simeon on top of his pillar and surrounded by a balustrade.

prayer, selflessness and justice. Many were converted to Christianity through his example, particularly among the nomadic peoples of the Syrian desert. After his death, Simeon's body was removed to Antioch for burial, but in about 480 Emperor Zeno began work on a vast pilgrimage church at Qal'at Si'man, whose octagonal crossing rose above Simeon's pillar.

Stephen *Died c.35* AD
First Christian martyr
Feast day December 26

Everything known about the life of Stephen is set out in chapters 6 and 7 of *Acts of the Apostles*. He was among the seven deacons chosen by the apostles to attend to the needs of the Hellenic widows among the early Christian community in Jerusalem, and was presumably a Greek-speaker himself. His preaching and miracle-working aroused the hostility of the Jews and he was denounced as a blasphemer and brought before the Sanhedrin. Here he delivered the great speech reported in *Acts* 7^{2-53}, summarizing the history of Israel and arguing that the Temple was impermanent, destined to be superseded by the coming of the prophet predicted by Moses, and that Jesus of Nazareth was this Christ. His speech ended by accusing the audience of being "stiff-necked and uncircumcized in heart and ears," and dominated by those who always resisted the Holy Spirit. The attack

clearly stung, for the trial was abandoned at this point and Stephen was taken outside and stoned to death, in accordance with the Mosaic prescription for transgressors, Saul (**St. Paul**) standing guard over the clothes of the stone-throwers.

Despite the attempts of fourth-century Christians to locate the whereabouts of Stephen, the tomb was not discovered until 415, after which the relics were translated to Constantinople where it seems likely that the body was broken up, for a fragment was almost certainly enshrined in the custom-built church of S. Stefano Rotundo, Rome between 468 and 483. The dispersal of the saint's remains, along with stones said to have been used at his martyrdom, was instrumental in popularizing the cult during the Middle Ages. By the eleventh century the cathedrals of Bourges, Sens and Auxerre possessed relics and had taken dedications to St. Stephen, while the great early medieval complex of monastic churches at Bologna, S. Stefano, also laid claim to portions of the saint.

Theresa of Ávila *1515-82*
Nun and mystic Feast day October 15

Born to an aristocratic Castilian family at Ávila and christened Teresa Sánchez de Cepeda y Ahumanda, Theresa was educated by Augustinian nuns and entered the Carmelite convent of the Incarnation at Ávila in 1535. Forced to return to her family the fol-

LEFT: *The Stoning of Stephen* (St-Germain-d'Auxerre, Yonne, France). The cult of Stephen the deacon was perhaps strongest in the early Middle Ages, though the paucity of documentation and poor survival rate of painting or sculpture make it difficult to assess how widespread such a cult may have been. This wall painting is one of three devoted to Stephen in the crypt of the abbey of St-Germain at Auxerre, and was probably commissioned during the reign of Emperor Charles the Bald to coincide with the translation of the relics of Germanus of Auxerre in 859.

RIGHT: *The Ecstasy of St. Theresa* (Gianlorenzo Bernini: Rome, Sta Maria della Vittoria). Bernini's altarpiece, carved between 1644 and 1647, derives from his reading of Theresa's meditation on prayer and spiritual life, *The Interior Castle*, and serves as a realization of the state Theresa described as "union."

lowing year after she fell ill with a persistent fever, possibly malaria, Theresa was received back into the convent in 1539, and until 1555 led a fairly convivial and relaxed life in a foundation famous in the town for its indulgent approach to the rules of enclosure. Her own writings identify a vision of 1555 in which she saw herself alongside two penitents, **Mary Magdalen** and **Augustine of Hippo**, as a turning-point, and thenceforth she experienced a series of "ecstasies," of which the mystical piercing of her heart by an arrow of divine love is the best known. She suffered much ridicule in the convent through these visions, but was supported by her confessor, the austere mystic Peter of Alcántara, and resolved to found a convent structured around the primitive Carmelite Rule.

The convent of St. Joseph at Ávila opened in 1562 as a house of discalced (barefooted) Carmelites, with a congregation of 13 nuns committed to a life of poverty, manual work and prayer. The same year also saw Theresa complete the writing of her *Life*, which she rapidly followed with her *Way of Perfec-*

tion, a tract intended for the instruction of nuns. In this she lays down a model for all reformed (discalced) Carmelite convents to follow. They were to be small, disciplined, hard-working, and staffed by intelligent and commonsensical nuns ("God preserve us from stupid nuns"). Theresa's co-operation with **John of the Cross** during the late 1560s led to the reform spreading to the male Carmelite friars. Her later life was spent supervising the growth of the reformed Order, and she died at Alba de Tormes (Castile) in 1582, while returning from the consecration of a new convent in Burgos.

Her meditation on prayer and the spiritual life, *The Interior Castle*, is perhaps the most profound to emerge out of sixteenth-century Europe, and it is here, more than in her conventual reforms, that her influence was greatest. One of the most important of her writings, the work amounts to an anatomy of prayer, distinguishing various states between contemplation ("quiet") and ecstasy ("union"), and was the first to recognize the life of prayer as manifold.

BELOW: This photograph of 1896 shows Thérèse Martin (or Theresa of Lisieux, far right), with three of her sisters and a cousin, all sisters at the Carmelite convent of Lisieux. From left to right they are; Marie Martin, Pauline Martin, Céline Martin and Marie Guérin.

Theresa of Lisieux *1873-97*
Carmelite nun Feast day October 1

Born to a conventionally pious family in Alençon, Theresa was the daughter of Louis Martin, a watchmaker, and Zélie Guérin. The family moved to Lisieux after the death of Theresa's mother in 1877, where she was raised in an atmosphere of deep religiosity by an aunt. Having already seen two of her sisters join the Carmelite convent in Lisieux, Theresa underwent at the age of 14 what she described as the complete conversion of her soul, and asked her father for permission to join her sisters on the rue Carmel. The Carmelites refused to accept so young a candidate, and it was not until she went on a pilgrimage to Rome that she obtained papal dispensation and joined the order in April, 1888, at the age of 15. It was a short vocation, undertaken "to save souls and, above all, to pray for the priests," but it had the heroic quality of a profoundly-experienced spiritual journey, and was recorded with stark fidelity in her *Histoire d'Une Ame*, finished a few days before her death in 1897.

Her cult is principally due to the decision of the prioress of the Carmelites at Lisieux to commission a heavily edited version of *L'Histoire d'Une Ame* from Theresa's sister, Agnes, and to circulate copies of this to other Carmelite houses. It was subsequently translated into most European languages and became a bestseller, precipitating a pilgrimage to the convent at Lisieux, particularly by the young. Theresa was canonized in 1925, and in 1929 the architect Le Cordonnier was commissioned to design the vast and hideous basilica of Ste-Thérèse which now dominates Lisieux, built to accommodate the increasing number of pilgrims to her shrine.

Thomas *First century*
Apostle Feast day July 3

Thomas is mentioned in all the gospels but given particular emphasis in *John*, where he is called "Didymus" (twin). John attests to both his skepticism and his impetuosity, recounting his suggestion that the disciples should die with Christ, and his interroga-

LEFT: Statue of Theresa of Lisieux asking her father's permission to join the Carmelite order. It stands in the garden of Les Buissonnets, the house in Lisieux to which the Martin family moved in 1877.

148

LEFT: *The Incredulity of St. Thomas*, by Giovanni Battista Cima. Cima's early sixteenth-century altarpiece places Thomas and the Resurrected Christ within a north Italian hall.

tion of Christ at the Last Supper: "Lord, we know not whither thou goest; and how can we know the way?" He is most celebrated for his refusal to believe in the Resurrection until he had "put my finger into the print of the nails, and thrust my hand into his side." His subsequent affirmation of the divinity of Christ, "my Lord and my God," is among the

most quoted confessions of faith of the Bible.

The *Acts of Thomas*, probably early third century, speak of Thomas' missionary work in Syria, and maintain that his journey was inspired by an invitation by Gundaphorus, a king of India, to design and build a palace for him. This forms the prelude to a tour of

southern India, where his preaching converted many before he was killed and buried at Mylapore, near Madras. The ancient Syrian Christian communities of Kerala (south-west India) certainly referred to themselves as "Christians of St. Thomas" well before Portuguese settlers began to arrive in the late fifteenth century, and point to a cross bearing a seventh-century Pahlavi inscription extoling St. Thomas at Mylapore as evidence of the longevity of the cult. Whatever the merits of the account, and the text is primarily written in the gnostic interest, it was widely accepted in the early Church, and the tradition that his body was translated from India to Edessa in Mesopotamia (modern Urfa, in south-eastern Turkey) chimes with the inauguration of his shrine there in 394.

Thomas Aquinas *c.1225-74*
Dominican theologian
Feast day January 28

Born at Rocca Secca (Latium) to the family of Count Landulf of Aquino, Thomas was educated at the Benedictine monastery of Monte Cassino. After a further four years at the university of Naples, and despite the opposition of his noble relatives, he joined the Dominican order in 1244 and was sent to study under Albertus Magnus in Paris, where he stayed from 1245-48. He joined Albertus in founding a center for Dominican study in Cologne and, returning to Paris in 1252, was appointed lecturer at the Dominican convent of St-Jacques, being awarded the title Master of Theology in 1256. The rest of his life was spent writing and teaching in Anagni, Orvieto, Rome, Viterbo, Paris, and Naples, before he died at Fossanova (Latium) on March 7, 1274, a vision of God having famously persuaded him to abandon work on his *Summa Theologica*: "All I have written seems to me like so much straw compared with what I have seen."

The philosophical and theological works of Thomas Aquinas are the most ambitious and comprehensive to emerge from the Middle Ages, and gave rise to a system of thought known as Thomism. At their heart lies a fundamental distinction between the claims of reason and of faith, and a methodology based on the application of Aristotelian logic to questions of doctrine and the interpretation of authority. Thomas was introduced to Aristotle's metaphysics by Albertus Magnus, but his rigor goes far beyond the work of his master or the re-

ABOVE: Thomas Aquinas defends the rights of the Mendicant Orders before Pope Alexander IV (engraving after a painting by Benozzo Gozzoli). Thomas Aquinas wrote his *Contra Impugnantes Dei Cultum* during his tenure as a lecturer at the Dominican convent of St-Jacques in Paris. The work was intended as a rebuttal of the criticisms of the Mendicant Orders then being voiced by the secular staff of the University of Paris, and was instrumental in promoting him as a spokesman for the new preaching orders. The engraving illustrated here portrays a debate between Thomas and the Parisian critics held at Anagni in 1256.

PREVIOUS PAGES: *The Apotheosis of St. Thomas Aquinas*, by Andrea da Firenze. This wall painting covers one of the side walls of the chapter house of the Dominican church of Sta Maria Novella in Florence, and dates from 1366-68. It forms part of a larger cycle commissioned by a wealthy merchant, Buonamico Guidalotti, a friend of the charismatic Dominican preacher, and one-time prior of Sta Maria, Jacopo Passavanti. Thomas Aquinas is represented surrounded by personifications of the Theological Sciences and Liberal Arts, while the Seven Virtues hover above his head. At his feet are the heretics Sabellius, Averroes, and Arius. The composition is rigidly doctrinaire, and is one of a number of affirmations of Dominican orthodoxy produced in the wake of the Black Death.

LEFT: Thomas the Apostle led to his martyrdom, nineteenth-century engraving.

ductionist approach of earlier scholastic philosophers such as Abelard. His most influential works were the dozen or so commentaries he wrote on the works of Aristotle and the major biblical scriptures, and his two enquiries into the philosophical basis for a belief in God, the *Summa Contra Gentiles* of *c.*1259-64 and *Summa Theologica* of 1266-73. The latter, though unfinished, became the classic theological textbook of the later Middle Ages, a magnificent compendium of statements, authorities, objections, reconciliations and conclusions on the vast majority of matters of concern for theology.

Thomas Becket *c.1118-70*
Archbishop and martyr
Feast day December 29.
Feast of the translation of relics July 7

Becket was born to a wealthy Anglo-Norman family in London, and was given the education of a nobleman in Merton and Paris. He joined the staff of Theobald, Archbishop of Canterbury, *c.*1142 and was promptly sent to study canon law in Bologna, followed by a spell in Auxerre. On his return Theobald ordained him deacon, and in 1154 appointed him archdeacon of Canterbury. This administrative position brought him to the attention of Henry II, newly acceded to the English throne, and in 1155, at Theobald's suggestion, Henry made Becket Chancellor of England. There then began a close friendship between the two, as Henry sought to govern his vast Plantagenet domains, reform the administration of justice, and persuade the baronage to swallow their local powers and surrender their castles. In all this he received shrewd and tireless support from Becket, and must have expected the same when, on Theobald's death in 1161, he nominated Becket as Archbishop of Canterbury. The monks at Canterbury probably viewed the situation very differently, for Becket had a reputation for restlessness, vanity, and high living. Nonetheless, Henry's wishes were accepted, and in 1162 Thomas Becket was formally installed as Archbishop of Canterbury.

Becket threw himself into his new position with an energy which terrified the monks, and irritated Henry from the very outset. He immediately resigned his post as Chancellor, to Henry's chagrin; adopted a monastic habit; and called for the canonization of **Anselm**. Next he prosecuted Canterbury's quite extremist claims to patronage and land, using the metropolitan sanction of excommunication against anyone who opposed his measures. Privately, he took to wearing a hair-shirt and secretly washing the feet of the poor each dawn. Becket's refusal to countenance the right of secular courts to try clerics accused of civil crimes was the last straw as far as Henry was concerned, and late in 1163 Henry circulated copies of his "grandfather's customs" to the bishops, asking them to approve the transfer of cases involving "criminous clerics" to secular courts. The following year these were formally codified as the Constitutions of Clarendon, but Becket denied their validity, and Henry issued a series of claims for substantial monies outstanding against Becket from his time as Chancellor. Shortly before Henry convened a council at Northampton to pass judgment on these claims, Becket fled the country and sought the protection of Pope Alexander III, then in Sens (Burgundy).

There followed six years of exile, while an increasingly acrimonious dispute with Henry raged. The issues were complex, and raised the whole question of the proper relations between Church and State, but the intense personal hostility felt by the main protagonists clouded any finer points at issue. Until 1166 Becket lodged at the Cistercian abbey of Pontigny (Burgundy), but Henry's threat to expel all Cistercians from England unless he moved persuaded Becket to seek sanctuary at the Benedictine abbey of Ste-Colombe, Sens, which lay under the direct protection of the French king, Louis VII. He spent most of his exile here, though there were meetings with Henry elsewhere, at Domfront (Normandy), for instance, in the winter of 1166. The low point was reached in 1169, when Henry had his eldest son, Henry Court-Mantel, crowned by Roger Pont-l'Evêque, Archbishop of York, thus breaching the prerogatives of Canterbury. Becket excommunicated Roger and threatened to place England under interdict. The bitterness finally subsided in August, 1170, after a party of papal legates managed to broker a settlement, in which Henry affirmed Canterbury's rights to conduct all coronations, and Becket sent simple letters of suspension to all bishops who had assisted Roger in York.

Becket returned to England on November 30, 1170, and made straight for Canterbury. Matters began to deteriorate when he refused to reinstate the bishops unless they

publicly swore an oath of obedience to the papacy, and came to a final pass in late December. Henry held his Christmas court of 1170 at Bures-sur-Dives, near Caen (Normandy), where reports of Becket's pronouncements at Canterbury were regularly received. The ultimate injury was probably Becket's choice of text for the Christmas sermon in Canterbury Cathedral, "Peace on Earth to Men of Goodwill." This prefaced a furious attack on his enemies – "may their memories be blotted out from the company of the saints" – and an equally angry outburst from Henry – "will no-one rid me of this low-born priest." Four knights, Hugues de Morville, Guillaume de Tracy, Reginald Fitz-Urse and Richard le Breton, made their way across the Channel, and on the afternoon of December 29 murdered Becket while he prayed in the north transept of Canterbury Cathedral.

ABOVE: *The Martyrdom of Thomas Becket*, prefatory miniature from a late twelfth-century psalter portraying Becket's murder.

That evening, while removing his garments, the monks discovered Becket's infested hair-shirt. They cleansed his body and placed it in the axial chapel of Anselm's crypt. Despite the circumstances of his death, it is unlikely that at this point the monks had any premonition that Becket would be acclaimed a saint. Indeed, as Frank Barlow argued in his recent biography of Becket (*Thomas Becket*, Los Angeles, 1986), "his rule as archbishop can be viewed as disastrous for all concerned." The miracles changed that, and within days of Becket's death dramatic cures at his tomb were being reported. One of the monks, Benedict of Peterborough (subsequently prior at Canterbury from 1175-77), was detailed to keep a tally, a sort of audit of miracles, which was continued by others after Benedict's removal to Peterborough; 703 were recorded by 1180. Matters began to move extremely quickly. On February 21, 1173, Pope Alexander III formally canonized Becket. On July 12, 1174, Henry II submitted to a symbolic penance in Canterbury Cathedral. On September 5, 1174 the old cathedral choir went up in flames. And between 1175 and 1184 a new and magnificent eastern arm, the largest in Europe, was constructed to house a monks' choir, Trinity Chapel and the Corona (or axial rotunda). The two latter areas were for Becket, and although his body was not formally translated into the Trinity Chapel until 1220, the pilgrimage was in full swing.

Ursula *Third century*
Virgin and martyr
Feast day October 21

Ursula's is a quite fantastical story, elaborated in many versions. Somewhere toward the beginning of the cult, there exists an inscription in the church of St. Ursula, Cologne, which recounts the restoration of a church by Clematius where virgin-martyrs had once shed their blood. The stone tooling of the inscription dates from *c.*400. The next surviving document is ninth century, and maintains that "many" virgins had fled to Cologne and were martyred for their faith by the Emperor Maximian, possibly during the late 280s. A late-ninth-century calendar mentions Ursula as one of several virgins martyred in Cologne, and a tenth-century account maintains that Ursula was one of 11,000 virgins massacered under Maximian. After that there was no stopping the embellishments.

LEFT: *Thomas Becket* (Sens Cathedral). This figure of an archbishop is now mounted beneath the Becket window in the north choir aisle of Sens Cathedral. The evidence for seeing the figure as Becket is admittedly circumstantial, but strong.

BELOW: *The Arrival of the Ambassadors*, by Vittore Carpaccio, detail from a cycle of the legend of St. Ursula painted for the Scuola di Sant'Orsola in Venice between 1490 and 1496. The scene shown here represents the ambassadors of King Conan demanding the betrothal of Ursula to Hereus (Etherius).

The most common form taken by the legend is that found in the *Golden Legend*. This makes Ursula the daughter of a British king, Maurus, who raised her as a Christian. Her reputation for wisdom and beauty was such that the pagan "King of England" demanded she be betrothed to his son, Etherius, but Ursula insisted that the marriage should be delayed for three years, during which time her suitor should be baptized into the faith, while she and ten other virgins might sail the seas. Eleven triremes were prepared and each virgin was granted a further thousand virgins as companions. At length the ships sailed up the Rhine to Cologne, where an angel foretold the women's eventual martyrdom, and on to Basel, where they abandoned the ships and traveled to Rome overland. Pope Cyriacus received them with honor, but when they returned to Cologne they found the city besieged by Huns, and were martyred in an orgy of violence outside the city walls. Other variations on the legend exist, often

quite local in character, as in Venice or Bruges, but the 1155 discovery of a mountain of bones in Cologne set the seal on what proved one of the most popular of all medieval legends to grace Lotharingia, the Rhineland, and northern France.

ABOVE: Swiss woodcut of *c*.1460 showing St. Ursula crowned as a Virgin, and shot with the arrow which one version sees as her cause of death.

Veronica *First century?*
Woman of Jerusalem Feast day July 12

A cloth bearing an image of the face of Christ is recorded as being in Rome from the eighth century onward, where it is described as the veil of Veronica. Giraldus Cambrensis, writing in the late twelfth century, suggested the word Veronica referred to the cloth, *Vera Icona*, meaning true image, but the popular accounts all attribute the procuring of this portrait to one Veronica. The story is first encountered in the fourth-century *Acts of Pilate*, where a woman of Jerusalem named Veronica was said to have wiped the sweat from the face of Christ while he carried the cross to Calvary. The cloth she used retained an image. Various attempts were subsequently made to identify the woman in this apocryphal story with the woman cured of an issue of blood (*Matthew* $9^{20\text{-}22}$). The whole thing is pure invention, but the desire to validate a particular image as not having been made by human hands offers a parallel to the *Mandylion*, an Eastern icon believed to have been miraculously printed on a veil for King Abgar. The image became popular in the thirteenth century, when a number of "Veronica Heads" were painted into psalters, and became more widespread in Europe after the cloth was translated into a new receptacle at Old St. Peter's in 1297.

LEFT: *St. Veronica*, by the fifteenth-century Netherlandish painter Hugo van der Goes. The robed female figure at prayer beneath the cross is more usually associated with donors in fifteenth-century Netherlandish altarpieces, but has here been used by van der Goes to focus attention on the role of St. Veronica as one involved in lamentation.

Vitus *Died c.303*
Martyr Feast day June 15

Probably born in the Roman province of Lucania (southern Italy), Vitus was martyred under Diocletian. Circumstantial evidence suggests the cult was quite early, but the earliest surviving mentions of Vitus are sixth century. The Latin accounts of his life are later still, and make Vitus the son of a

LEFT: *The Veronica Head* (Evesham Psalter). Representations of the Veronica Head, the image impressed upon the cloth which Veronica used to wipe the head of Christ on the road to Calvary, became popular in thirteenth-century England, where they were intended as pictures for contemplation. The majority are to be found in psalters, as in this example of *c.*1250.

pagan family who was secretly raised in the Christian faith by his nurse, Crescentia, and her husband, Modestus. The cult took on a wider appeal after some relics of Vitus were translated to the abbey of Corvey (Westphalia) in 836, where they proved particularly useful in curing nervous disorders. As such, Vitus was considered the protector of those suffering from epilepsy, snake-bites, or convulsive fits, a group of which (the family of pathological diseases given the umbrella term *chorea*) became known as St. Vitus' Dance. The cult was strongest in southern Italy, Germany and Bohemia, where the late medieval cathedral at Prague took a dedication to St. Vitus.

Werburgh
Died late seventh century
Abbess Feast day February 3

Werburgh was the daughter of Wulfhere, King of Mercia, and was probably born *c*.650. The contemporary records are silent, and most of what is known is derived from the *Liber Eliensis* and a late-eleventh-century *Vita* written by Goscelin, probably while he was a monk at Canterbury. According to these traditions, Werburgh retired to her great-aunt **Etheldreda**'s monastery at Ely after her father died in 670. She spent the rest of what seems a relatively short life establishing new monastic houses in Mercia – Weedon (Northamptonshire), Hanbury (Staffordshire), and Threckingham (Lincolnshire) among them – and died at Threckingham, perhaps as early as 685. Her body was removed to Hanbury for burial, but some time between 893 and 907, Werburgh was translated to the Anglo-Saxon minster at Chester by Aethelflaed, Queen of Mercia.

The fact of this translation suggests that considerable importance was attached to the cult of St. Werburgh, for Aethelflaed's move was part of a broader strategy to establish Chester as an Anglo-Saxon bulwark against the Danes, and is broadly contemporary with her translation of the remains of the Northumbrian king and martyr, Oswald, to Gloucester. The minster was in turn refounded as a Benedictine abbey in 1093, on the advice of **Anselm**, and its dedication to St. Werburgh was retained. Goscelin's *Vita* was probably written to coincide with this refoundation, but despite his use of testimony from Weedon, it is largely legendary. The most celebrated story, Werburgh's resurrection of a goose eaten by a Weedon villager, is a straight borrowing from the life of the eighth-century Flemish nun, Amelburga. Nonetheless the cult of St. Werburgh was sufficiently attractive to persuade the monks at Chester to commission a new shrine in about 1340, whose rare and beautiful base survives in the Lady Chapel of what is now Chester Cathedral.

William of York *Died 1154*
Archbishop Feast day June 8

Born into a noble family related to that of King Stephen, William was known in his own lifetime as William fitz Herbert. He was appointed treasurer to the Chapter of York, perhaps as early as 1130, and chaplain to King Stephen after the latter ascended to the throne in 1135. In 1142 the York Chapter elected William Archbishop of York, following considerable pressure from King Stephen, but the appointment was bitterly opposed by **Bernard of Clairvaux** and the monks at Fountains, who accused William of simony. Theobald, Archbishop of Canterbury, refused to consecrate William, and the dispute was referred to Rome, where Innocent II ruled the appointment valid on condition the accusations leveled by Richard II, abbot of Fountains, were denied on oath by William and the dean of York.

William was finally consecrated archbishop in 1143 by his uncle, Henry of Blois, Bishop of Winchester, and the dispute might have been resolved then and there, but for the dean of York's insistence that his oath should be sworn not by him, but on his behalf. From a Cistercian point of view this was no solution at all, and after Henry Murdac, a personal friend of Bernard of Clairvaux, was appointed abbot of Fountains in 1144, letters were sent to most European prelates denouncing William's consecration as fraudulent. William was summoned to Rome following the election of Pope Eugenius III, a Cistercian, in 1145, and arrived in 1147 to be informed he was suspended. His supporters sacked the abbey of

ABOVE: The St. Werburgh shrine base, from a watercolor by the nineteenth-century English artist Samuel Prout. Between 1635 and 1876 the mid-fourteenth-century base of the shrine of St. Werburgh was incorporated into the bishop's throne, and situated on the south side of the choir of Chester Cathedral. Prout's watercolor of *c.*1847 illustrates the bizarre arrangement which resulted.

Fountains shortly afterward, on which news William was deposed at the Council of Reims and Henry Murdac, his bitter opponent, was consecrated archbishop in his stead. William retreated to Winchester, where he was sheltered by Henry of Blois, joined the monastic priory and led a life of exemplary austerity. Matters only changed in 1153, when Henry Murdac, Bernard of Clairvaux and Pope Eugenius III all died within a few months of each other. Pope Anastasius IV restored William to York, and William in turn promised to recompense Fountains for the damage it had suffered. A month after his 1154 return to York, however, he died suddenly and unexpectedly, quite probably poisoned.

William was buried in the cathedral, where he seems to have become regarded as a martyr, and by the late twelfth century miracles began to be reported at his tomb. He was eventually canonized in 1227, a locally popular cult which answered a definite need, given the tremendous explosion of interest in reliquary cults on the part of thirteenth-century English chapters. Prior to William, all York's sainted archbishops were enshrined elsewhere, John at Beverley, Wilfrid at Ripon, Oswald at Worcester, Paulinus at Rochester. William filled the gap, and was celebrated in the commissioning of a superb new shrine base c.1330, and a justly famous miracle window in 1421.

Wulfstan c.1009-95
Bishop Feast day January 19

Born at Long Itchington (Warwickshire) and educated in the monastic schools at Evesham and Peterborough, Wulfstan moved to Worcester c.1034, where he was ordained priest by Bishop Brihteah, and entered the cathedral priory as a monk shortly afterward. Thereafter he served as sacristan and prior until Bishop Aldred's elevation to the archbishopric of York created a vacancy, and Edward the Confessor approved Wulfstan's appointment as Bishop of Worcester in 1062.

Wulfstan's episcopate coincided with the Norman Conquest and the subsequent reform of the English Church. Remarkably for an Anglo-Saxon prelate, and particularly one whose relations with King Harold were such that he negotiated with the Northumbrian earls on his behalf, Wulfstan developed a good working relationship with the new Norman settlers. He openly supported the decrees of the 1075 Council of London,

and **though** his relations with Lanfranc (Archbishop of Canterbury, 1070-89) were initially complicated by Worcester's historical relationship with York, Wulfstan accepted Lanfranc's ruling that his see was a suffragan of Canterbury. Co-operation between the two became close during the late 1070s, and together they should be given the credit for extinguishing the Anglo-Irish slave trade. His administration of the diocese was also much admired by Lanfranc, who noted the enthusiasm with which he encouraged the foundation of new parish churches, assiduously visited all areas under his control, and bravely attempted to enforce clerical celibacy.

Although he shed tears at the demolition of the Anglo-Saxon church, Wulfstan approved the building of a new cathedral at Worcester in 1084, whose choir was sufficiently advanced for the monks to take up residence in 1089. His presidency of a synod in the crypt of this church in 1092 was the last major event in Wulfstan's life, and in 1095, by then in his eighties and one of the very last Anglo-Saxon-born churchmen to hold high office, he died. He was buried in his new cathedral, and within a few years the first cures were reported at his tomb. This tomb was described by William of Malmesbury, writing in the 1120s: "It lies between two *piramides* vaulted over above with a beautiful stone arch. A wooden beam projects out above, which has fixed in it iron grills, which are called spiders' webs." Wulfstan's formal canonization only took place in 1203, but the cult was popular from the time of his death, and remained so until the destruction of the shrine by Henry VIII's commissioners in 1538.

BELOW: King John's tomb (Worcester Cathedral). In 1232 King John was placed in a new sarcophagus in front of the main altar of Worcester Cathedral and close to the shrines of Wulfstan and Oswald. The position was prestigious, to say the least, but even more startlingly, images of two bishops, Wulfstan and Oswald again, were carved to either side of John's head, commending the dead king to God. The detail chosen here illustrates one of the two sained bishops (which is Wulfstan and which Oswald is unclear) with John's head to the left.

Acknowledgments

The publisher would like to thank designer David Eldred. We should also like to thank the following institutions, agencies and individuals for supplying photographic material.

AA Photo Library: page 46
AKG, London: page 32
Courtesy of the Benedictine Convent of St. Hildegard, Rudesheim-Eibingen: page 76
Bettmann Archive, New York: pages 4, 7, 11 both, 15 both, 16 both, 17, 25 top, 27, 30, 34 bottom, 36, 37, 38, 39 top, 40, 42 top, 45, 48, 50, 51, 52, 53 top, 57, 61, 64, 66, 70, 71, 74, 75 all, 80, 82, 84, 85, 91 top, 94, 100 both, 104, 106, 107, 110, 112, 114 both, 121 both, 122, 126, 127 top, 128, 130 bottom, 131 top, 133, 137 bottom, 143, 146, 149, 152, 155 top, 156 top
Bibliothèque Municipale, Poitiers: page 138
The Board of Trinity College, Dunblin: page 12
British Library, London: pages 3, 10, 59, 124, 153, 156 bottom
British Museum, London: page 98
Cartuja de Miraflores, Burgos: 79
Courtesy of the Conservateur des Antiquités et Objets d'Art, St-Julien Cathedral, Le Mans: page 72 both
The Dean and Chapter of Durham Cathedral: page 42 bottom
Courtesy of the Dean and Chapter of Westminster: page 135
Giraudon, Paris: page 77
Haskins, Susan: page 120 top
Life File, London: pages 13 (photo Andrew Ward), 31 (photo Terry O'Brien), 69 bottom (photo Emma Lee), 123 (photo Andrew Ward), 157 (Photo Emma Lee), 159 (by kind permission of the Dean and Chapter, Worcester, photo Terry O'Brien)
McCleneghan, Daniel: page 131 bottom
Mackenchnie-Jarvis, Mr. J.P.: page 14
McNeill, John: pages 9 bottom left, 18 bottom, 87, 115, 127 bottom, 129 right, 130 top, 139, 154 top
MAS, Barcelona: pages 81, 96, 125
The Master and Fellows of Corpus Christi College, Cambridge: page 24
The Master and Fellows of University College, Oxford: page 44
Musée de l'Abbaye St-Germain, Auxerre/Cliché Hervé: page 144
Musée des Beaux-Arts, Dijon: page 99
Musées departementaux de la Seine-Maritime, photo François Dugue: page 94 top
National Gallery, London: pages 1, 26, 29 bottom, 35, 55, 60 bottom, 73, 92, 93, 141, 142, 148
Courtesy Pélérinage Sainte Thérèse de Lisieux: page 147
Photo Resources, Canterbury, Kent: pages 6, 9 top and bottom right, 18 top, 29 top, 34 top, 39 bottom, 53 bottom, 54, 60 top, 66, 88, 90, 95 bottom, 108, 109 top, 120 bottom, 129 left, 132, 134, 137 top
Private Collection, Gloucestershire, photo Nick Nicholson: page 56
Reproduced by permission of Cheshire County Council Archives and Local Studies Service: page 158
Scala, Florence: 2, 19, 20/21, 22/23, 25 bottom, 41, 43, 58, 62/63, 68-69, 86, 102, 105, 109 bottom, 111, 113, 116, 117, 136, 140, 145, 150/151, 154/155
Sonia Halliday Photographs: 49, 97, 103
Städelsches Kunstinstitut, Frankfurt: page 28
Szépmüvézeti Museum, Budapest: page 83